A
COMPANION
TO
PIRKE AVOT

A
COMPANION
TO
PIRKE AVOT

Rabbi Benjamin Morgenstern

gefen נכ

A COMPANION TO PIRKEI AVOT

Rabbi Benjamin Morgenstern

©Benjamin Morgenstern
Jerusalem 5743/1983
All Rights Reserved

Typeset by Gefen Ltd.
Bet-El D.N. Jerusalem Hills
90300 Israel

ISBN 965-229-008-4

PRINTED IN ISRAEL

All in whom man takes delight the
Almighty takes delight.

(Ethics 3:13)

**Dedicated to the memory of
Louis J. Schreiber**

Who in his life-time personified the
three basic principles on which the
world is based;
Torah-Divine worship and Acts of
loving kindness.

(Ethics 1:2)

CONTENTS

CONTENTS

Acknowledgements

Rabbi Benjamin Morgenstern was not only a very effective preacher and pastor during those decades he served his congregation in Brooklyn, New York, but was also an educator, teacher and administrator - of unusual excellence. As an educator he fathomed the need to make important texts vivid and relevant, so that students, both young and old, would be able to remember them and apply them in daily life.

He has applied this very technique to the ever popular tractate of the Mishna, Pirke Avot, in this volume. His extensive research in Talmudic and Midrashic literature, searching for the historic background for the application of these cherished maxims is indeed comprehensive. The result is a most readable and useful companion for the study of the ancient text. For this he merits our profoundest gratitude.

Professor Emanuel Rackman
President, Bar-Ilan University

In the current volume "A Companion to Pirke Avot", Rabbi Morgenstern interprets the doctrine of some of the greatest Mishnaic teachers of Judaism in light of the actual events of their time. He thus revives their personalities for the reader and helps him gain unique insight into the era in which they lived. He discusses the struggles and problems of those periods with much originality and endeavors to portray the Sages' response to the challenges of their times. The Pirke Avot gain new relevancy through this work.

Professor Eliezer Berkovitz
Chairman Emeritus Dept. of
Jewish Philosophy,
Hebrew Theological College,
Skokie, Ill.

Introduction

In the forty years of my life which I spent in the pulpit-rabbinate, ten years with the Young Israel of Mapleton Park and thirty years in the Congregation Sons of Israel of Bensonhurst, one of my favorite activities was the regular lesson that I taught in Tractate Avot, or Pirkei Avot, Ethics of the Fathers as it is popularly known.

A chapter of Avot is read every Shabbat at the Mincha service from Pesach to Rosh Ha-Shanah. These summer Shabbat afternoons spent teaching and discussing Avot are among my most pleasant memories.

The philosophy and wisdom contained in Avot is as relevant today as it was when the various aphorisms were first stated. The vast number of volumes that have been written and are still being written today in commentary to Avot, can be discussed and considered from as many angles as there are sparks shooting out of the blacksmith's anvil. They are true maxims of wisdom and as such contain level over level of profound thought. Only after the determined climber reaches one peak of understanding does he realize that there are still other peaks for him to reach.

Pirkei Avot is basically a description of the chain of tradition through which the oral Law, Torah She-Be'al Peh, was handed down from Moses at Mt. Sinai until the redaction of the Mishnah by Rabbi Judah Hanasi in approximately 220 C.E. We are told which sage received the tradition from whom, and we are given his favorite or outstanding dicta. Some of the sayings are very terse and even laconic; others are fuller and more detailed. There can be no doubt that *many if not most of the sayings were occasioned by something that happened in which the sage was involved as a principal or as an observer. It was not the custom of our Sages to offer systematic presentations of their philosophies. They were far too occupied dealing with real life in the form of mitzvot and ma'asim tovim to devote their time to sterile speculation. A knowlege of the circumstances that might have occasioned a specific aphorism, and an acquaintance with the personality of the author and the historical background of his life, can add a great deal to our understanding and enjoyment of his words of wisdom as we read them in Avot.*

That is the purpose of this work. It is not a commentary on Avot but rather A Companion to it. The sources from which the information is culled are the traditional works of rabbinical literature such as the Babylonian and Jerusalem Talmuds, (J.T.) the various Midrashim, and the classical commentators. Only rarely have I used "outside" sources such as Josephus.

For those readers who want to examine the sources directly - something which I most wholeheartedly recommend - I have given detailed references at the end of each chapter. Because this work is concerned with the Avot themselves, i.e., the rabbis, each chapter concerns a specific rabbi. The chapters are arranged in the order of the rabbis' appearance in Pirkei Avot. Three sages, Menachem, Rabban Gamaliel of Yavneh and Rabbi Natan the Babylonian have been included though they are not cited in Avot. They have been inserted in their chronological order. The reason for this inclusion will be clear from the chapters discussing the exalted positions that they held in the Sanhedrin.

During my years in the rabbinate I was too busy teaching, counseling and preaching to find time for writing. Many devoted congregants constantly pleaded with me to commit my classes, lectures and sermons to writing, but I found little time to do so. "they made me the keeper of the vineyards, my own vineyard I did not plant," (Song of Songs 1:6). Since my retirement to Jerusalem I have begun to accede to that request. This is my first offering.

One of the pleasant duties of an author is to acknowlege the encouragement he has received. My association with Harav Hagaon, Rabbi Abraham Kroll Shelitah, of Jerusalem has been and continues to be a most inspiring association. He has always been ready to give of his limited time to discuss ideas and difficult sources, and more than once have I included his interpretations in this work. Dr. Raphael Posner edited the original manuscript and I am grateful for his constructive and valuable comments. To Dr. Dan Vogel, my sincere thanks for reading and commenting on many of the chapters.

To my Rabbinic colleagues, who have been a most faithful sounding board, for my analysis and interpretations, I humbly say, "todah rabbah".

Producing a book nowadays is a formidable undertaking, and I would like to acknowledge my appreciation to;
Dr. Saul & Elaine Schreiber of Phoenix, Arizona.
Gerald & Merle Kreditor of London, England.
David & Zelda Pomson of London, England.
George & Shirley Weinstein of Milwaukee, Wisc.
whose kind help has made this publication possible.

A special thanks to my grandchildren Rhoda and Natan Golan for their painstaking reviewing of the galley proofs.

Acharon, Acharon, chaviv. That the last mentioned in any list, is the most beloved, is a well established principle. In this context, I refer to my dear devoted wife Sylvia (Syd), who has indeed been a true helpmate. Every individual encounters difficult moments and situations in life, especially a person in the public eye. How much more so a Rabbi. She has never failed to encourage and assist me in all of my endeavors. What I owe her is beyond my capacity to express in words. I humbly and most sincerely thank her.

Writing this "Companion" to Avot has given me a great deal of personal gratification and satisfaction. If it adds a thought to your understanding of the tractate Pirkei Avot, I will have my full reward.

Jerusalem
Ellul 5742.

Rabbi B. Morgenstern

שִׁמְעוֹן הַצַּדִּיק הָיָה מִשְׁיָרֵי כְּנֶסֶת הַגְּדוֹלָה. הוּא הָיָה אוֹמֵר: עַל
שְׁלֹשָׁה דְּבָרִים הָעוֹלָם עוֹמֵד: עַל הַתּוֹרָה, וְעַל הָעֲבוֹדָה, וְעַל
גְּמִילוּת חֲסָדִים.

*Simeon the Tzaddik was one of the last (members) of the
Great Assembly. He used to say: 'The world stands on three
things: Torah; Avodah-Divine Worship; Gemilut Hasadim -
The practice of charity.'*[1]

The Second Temple existed for 420 years and in that time no
less than 300 High Priests served in the sanctuary. This gives an
average term of office of approximately one and one-half years
for each imcumbent. Simeon the Tzaddik, however, served as
High Priest for 40 years,[2] and his period of office is considered
by the sages to have been one of the most blessed for the Jewish
people.

The appellation, Tzaddik, is a rare one and it indicates the
immense respect and love which the rabbis of the Talmud felt
towards Simeon. That his contemporaries also harbored such
feelings is clear from the panegyric written by Simeon ben
Sira, the author of the apocryphal work, 'The words of Simeon
ben Sira' (or *Ecclesiasticus*, as it is also known). A whole
chapter[3] is devoted to Simeon ben Johanan, the High Priest,
who is Simeon the Tzaddik, extolling his contribution to the
welfare of the Temple, Jerusalem and the Jewish people and
the manner in which he performed his duties in the Temple:

Great among his bretheren and the glory of his people was
Simeon the son of Johanan, the High Priest, in whose

time the Temple was renovated... in whose days a cistern was dug holding an enormous amount of water... the wall of the Temple was built... who watched over his people against oppressors and protected his city against enemies...

How glorious was he... when he came out of the Sanctuary! Like a morning star from between the clouds and like the full moon on the festivals...

It is on this chapter in Ben Sira that the *piyyut, Mareh Kohen* ('The Appearance of the High Priest'), read in the Yom Kippur service, was based.

The sages of the Talmud describe a series of miracles which occurred regularly during the years that Simeon served as High Priest.[4]

One of the main duties of the *Kohen Gadol* was the performance of the rituals of Yom Kippur, the Day of Atonement. Of these perhaps the most important was the one of the goat to be sacrificed on the altar in the Temple and the one to be sent to Azazel, the mountain in the desert from which the goat was thrown down 'bearing the sins of Israel.' The selection procedure was as follows: Two identical goats were brought before the High Priest together with a container in which there were two plaques - one marked 'To God' and the other, 'To Azazel.' The High Priest inserted both his hands and drew out one of the plaques in each hand. If the one marked 'To God' was in his right hand, it was considered an extremely favorable omen. In each of the 40 Yom Kippur services at which Simeon presided, 'To God' came up in his right hand! After Simeon's death, the laws of chance took over.

Similarly, during Simeon's high-priesthood the red ribbon which was tied to the horn of the goat sent to Azazel always turned white before the goat had fallen half-way down the mountain. This too was considered to be a sign that God had forgiven Israel's sins as it is written, 'Though your sins be as scarlet, they will become as white as snow' (Isaiah 1:18). After

Simeon's death, some years the ribbon turned white and on others it remained red.

Another miracle which occurred regularly during Simeon's term of office had to do with the *Menorah,* the golden candelabrum in the Temple. The seven oil containers were filled daily with identical amounts of oil and the wicks were lit starting from the end wick to the west. During Simeon's incumbency, that light burned longer than all the others although it was the first to be kindled. This too was seen as a sign of God's presence.

By law, the altar had to be stoked with two logs every day and more were added as required. When Simeon was High Priest the two logs always lasted all day notwithstanding the number of offerings burned on the altar.

Finally, during all the 830 years of the two Temples, only seven (or, according to some, nine) Red Heifers were discovered for the purification rituals described in the Torah (Numbers 19:2). Of these, two were found and prepared according to the law during Simeon's tenure of office.[5]

The Talmud[6] also tells us that Simeon was aware on the Yom Kippur before his death that it would be his last. He explained this premonition by the fact that every year, when he entered the Holy of Holies on Yom Kippur, a man dressed in white accompanied him and left with him. On that Yom Kippur, however, the man was dressed in black and did not leave with him. From this Simeon understood that that Yom Kippur was to be his last and, indeed, seven days after the Sukkot festival he died. After his death, the other priests ceased to recite the Priestly Blessing using the full, ineffable Divine Name because, without Simeon, they felt themselves unworthy.

From the account of these and other miracles in the Talmud, the impression is given that the sages were convinced that the peace and prosperity which Simeon's generation enjoyed was due to his presence in its midst. He was a true *tzaddik* - a man of extreme piety who loved and protected the people he led.

In the Talmud there is mention of two High Priests called Simeon the Tzaddik - one was the grandfather of the other. Historians are divided on the question of which Simeon is referred to in the Talmudical sources, particularly with regard to the meeting with Alexander the Great (see below). We have taken the position that it was the grandfather.

Simeon's aphorism in our *mishnah* raises a question. When the Jews returned to Eretz Israel from Babylon led by Ezra the Scribe, they set up a court, or ruling council, called *Ha-Knesset Ha-Gedolah,* the Great Assembly. This body, which consisted of 120 members and was presumably presided over by the High Priest, constituted the spiritual and temporal government of Eretz Israel and, in effect, it laid the basis for Judaism as we know it today.

According to the Talmud[7], the body was called the Great Assembly because 'it restored greatness to its proper place' in that it inserted the word 'great' in the description of the Almighty found in the first benediction of the *Amidah* prayer. The men of the Great Assembly, however, did far more than that. They instituted and formulated the benedictions, the prayers and the various forms of *Kiddush* and *Havdalah*[8], and also redacted the *Midreshei Halakhah,* the legal *midrashim* to the Torah which are one of the foundations of the Oral Law[9]. Furthermore, the Great Assembly closed the canon of the Bible and even committed the books of Ezekiel, the Twelve Latter Prophets, Daniel and Esther to writing[10]. In *Avot D' Rabbi Natan*[11] we are told that 'in the beginning they used to say that Proverbs, Song of Songs and Ecclesiastes should be put away (i.e., excluded from the canon of the Bible) until the Men of the Great Assembly came and explained them.'

In Avot[12] we read that the prophets transmitted the Torah to the Men of the Great Assembly who said three things: 'Be deliberate in judgement; raise up many disciples; and make a fence around the Torah.' These instructions were guidelines for judges and rabbinical leaders and constituted the principles on which the Great Assembly operated. The Mishnah does not record the sayings of any individual members of the Assembly and, indeed, they have remained anonymous to the present day. Why was Simeon the Tzaddik singled out to be the only member in whose name an aphorism, is cited?

The answer to this question is to be found in the introductory statement in our *mishnah*. Simeon, as High Priest, was *ex officio* the president of the Great Assembly and presumably when the *mishnah* states that he was 'one of the last (members of the Great Assembly), it means that he was the last president before the Assembly ceased to exist and its place was taken by the Sanhedrin, which was led first by Antigonus of Sokho and then by the *Zugot* (the pairs of rabbis) in whose names the Mishnah continues to cite aphorisms. Thus, Simeon marks an important turning point in Jewish history and, as such, had to be mentioned by name. Since he was mentioned, the *mishnah* also recorded his favorite aphorism: 'The world stands on three things: *Torah; Avodah* and *Gemilut Hasadim*.' In a sense this statement is supplementary to the principles of the Men of the Great Assembly. They laid down guidelines for the reestablishment of the Jewish state and its judiciary; Simeon taught how the state could be maintained.

During Simeon's period of office, a major event in Jewish history took place. Alexander the Great came to conquer Eretz Israel but was himself conquered by the venerable Simeon, without an arrow being shot. The story is recorded in the Talmud[13] and by the historian, Josephus[14], but in the latter's account the High Priest is identified as Jadua.

Alexander had conquered Tyre and Gaza and turned his attention to Judea intending to teach it a lesson for not having answered his request for men and supplies during his Persian campaign. The Jews had remained loyal to Darius, the Persian emperor, to whom they had sworn an oath of allegiance, because the Persians had given them permission to rebuild the Temple and establish an autonomous government.

Although Judea was a small country and had no military significance at that time, Alexander was determined to make an example out of this issue so that all other nations should learn that when Alexander the Great requests – you comply! Alexander had, therefore, promised his soldiers and mercenaries a free hand in looting and despoiling Judea[15].

It must have been in great fear and terror that the Jews turned to Simeon to intercede with the Almighty lest the Temple be once again laid waste and the population massacred. Simeon offered sacrifices in the Temple and was granted a dream in which he was told to take courage as no harm would come from the Greek's visit. The Talmud[16] gives the following account of the meeting between Simeon the Tzaddik and Alexander the Great:

The twenty fifth of Tebet is the day of Mt. Gerizim on which no mourning is permitted. It is the day on which the Cutheans (Samaritans) demanded the House of our G-d from Alexander the Macedonian so as to destroy it, and he had given them the permission. Whereupon some people came and informed Simeon the Just, 'What did the latter do?' He put on his priestly garments. Some of the noblemen of Israel went with him carrying fiery torches in their hands, walked all night until the dawn rose. When the dawn rose, Alexander said to the Cutheans who were with him, 'Who are They'? The Cutheans answered: 'The Jews who rebelled against you'. When he reached Antipatris (near Kfar Saba) the sun having shone forth, they met. When Alexander saw Simeon the Just, he descended from his chariot and bowed down before him. They said to him, 'A great King, should bow down before this Jew'? Alexander answered, 'It was his image that won for me all my battles.' Alexander said to Simeon, 'What have you come for'? Simeon responded, 'Is it possible that star-worshippers should mislead you to destroy the House wherein prayers are said for you and your kingdom that it never be destroyed!' Alexander asked, 'and who are they?' 'They are the Cutheans who stand before you.' Alexander proclaimed, 'They are delivered into your hands.' The Jews destroyed the Cuthean temple on Mount Gerizim, even as they wanted to do to the House of G-d and that day was declared a holiday.

The Talmud tells us that Alexander went to Jerusalem and visited the Temple where he offered many sacrifices in thanksgiving for his successful campaigns. He did want to have a statue of himself erected in the Temple but desisted when he was told that Jewish law categorically forbade any image. However, Simeon promised that in his honor every male child born that year would be named for him. Thus Alexander became a Jewish name.

Alexander was so impressed with what Simeon taught concerning Judaism and the Torah way of life, that he granted the Jews many privileges, even exemption from taxes in Sabbatical Years. He called for young Jews to join his army and offered them estates in the countries he conquered and the right to practice their religion both in the army and their new settlements.[17]

Alexander was anxious to learn the laws, customs and ceremonies of the Jews and asked his hosts many questions. He wanted to know the Torah attitude to all sorts of problems that had occupied the minds of the Greek philosophers who had educated him in his childhood and youth and it is very possible that Simeon's terse aphorism recorded in our *mishnah* constitutes the main headings of his response to Alexander.

Nearly the whole of the known world at that time had been conquered by Alexander. A young man – he was only 33 years old when he died – he was totally confident in his own power and saw himself as the supreme ruler of the world. Furthermore, under the influence of Persian culture, he viewed himself as a god. Simeon, therefore, taught him about Torah, the constitution for mankind handed down by the Supreme

King of Kings, Almighty God. The proud Greek was confronted with a completely different *weltanshauung* which puts human beings - even the great Alexander - into their proper place in the universe.

Alexander worshiped every idol he came across in his vast conquered territories - idols of wood, stone or metal. It was his policy to adopt the gods of each conquered nation as his own to show tolerance and friendship. He was unable to understand the Jewish attitude - there were no idols in the Temple. The concept of a Supreme Being who cannot be seen or touched was beyond him. Simeon taught Alexander that *Avodah,* the worship of the one true God, is the only basis for the world. Until all the peoples of the world recognize the Almighty and serve Him there can be no harmony in the world. In addition to its intrinsic falsehood, idolatry is the main cause of division and conflict

The Greeks - and later the Romans - worshiped physical strength. They believed in the survival of the fittest and the destruction of the weak. Might is right! The Jews, however, are 'merciful people, the children of merciful people' and the Torah is replete with rules to govern human conduct; to protect the poor, the aged, the sick, the orphan, the widow and the other weak layers of society. Jewish law even protects dumb animals from unnecessary pain. In contrast, the Greeks loved physical struggles and their successors, the Romans, gave the world the 'sport' of gladiators destroying each other for the entertainment of the masses and the spectacle of innocent men, women and children being thrown to wild beasts to satiate the mob's thirst for blood.

Torah, Avodah and *Gemilut Hasadim* are indeed the pillars on which the welfare of society rests and we can well imagine that they were the major themes in Simeon's conversations with Alexander. Unfortunately, neither Alexander nor his successors learned Simeon's lessons.

Because of Alexander's conquests, Hellenistic culture spread throughout the world, and more and more individuals in Eretz Israel were affected by it. These people demanded the 'modernization' of religious practices and, in reaction, the Jews who remained loyal to their traditions became stricter and stricter in their application of the law. Many began to take the Nazirite vows and lived according to the very strict regimen that these vows involved. They refrained from wine and, in effect, removed themselves from normal social life. Simeon objected to this extremism just as he objected to the reforms the Hellenists were instituting. A clear indication of Simeon's attitude is the following story which he himself told:[18]

Simeon the Tzaddik said: I have never eaten of the guilt-offering of a defiled Nazirite except in the case of one man who came to me from the south. He was a handsome man with beautiful eyes and his hair was arranged in curls. I said to him 'My son! Why do you want to destroy such beautiful hair (the Nazirite being required to shave his head at the end of the period of the vow or if he becomes unclean during it)?' He said to me, 'I was working as a shepherd for my father in our town and once, when I went to draw water from the spring, I looked at my image in the water and my evil inclination gripped me so violently that it nearly drove me from the world! I said to it (the evil inclination or himself), 'Worthless one! Why are you so vain in a world which is not yours?! Your end will be corruption and worms! I swear that I will cut you (the hair) off for the sake of heaven!'' I kissed him on the head and told him, 'Such as you (i.e., with a good reason), may there be many Nazirites!'

Simeon the Tzaddik represents the ideal Jewish leader who is concerned for both the religious and material well-being of the people. Just as a three-legged stool cannot stand if even one of its legs is missing, so too the world cannot exist if any one of the principles on which it rests—*Torah, Avodah,* and *Gemilut Hasadim*—is not adequately developed and observed.

We can now understand Simeon's dictum. When it became
known that Alexander the Great was advancing toward Israel
to do battle against the Jews they must have come to Simeon in
great fear. "How can we hope to stand up against the mighty
forces of the Macedonians"? Simeon must have comforted
them by stating, "You fulfill your obligations to study Torah,
to offer sacrifices and prayers, to perform acts of Gemilut
Hassadim, in other words carry on as truly observant Jews are
required to live. As for the impending battle that faces us,
remember when the Jews were confronted with the Egyptians
persuing them prior to their crossing the Red Sea, Moses
proclaimed, "The Almighty will do battle for you and you can
be silent" (Exodus 14:14). Once again because of the virtuous
way of life that Israelites observed under Simeon's direction
of Torah, Mitzvot and Maasim Tovim, the Almighty indicated
his profound satisfaction and performed for them a great
miracle. Alexander the Great submitted to the Lordship of
Simeon the Tzaddik.

So may we formulate our lives and may we behold in our day
and in our time similar miracles.

NOTES

1. *Avot* 1:2
2. *Yoma* 9a, 39a
3. *The Words of Simeon ben Sira* Ch.50
4. *Yoma* 39a
5. *Parah* 3:5
6. *Yoma* 39b
7. *TJ Megillah* 3:7; *Yoma* 69b
8. *Berakhot* 33a
9. *TJ Shekalim* 5:1
10. *Bava Batra* 15a
11. *Avot D'Rabbi Natan* 1:4

12. *Avot* 1:1
13. *Yoma* 69a. See also *Tamid* 32a and *TJ Bava Metzia* 2:5
14. Josephus, *Antiquities* 11:8
15. Josephus, *ibid*
16. *Yoma* 69a
17. Josephus, *ibid*
18. *Nazir* 4b

Antigonus of Sokho

ג אַנְטִיגְנוֹס אִישׁ סוֹכוֹ קִבֵּל מִשִּׁמְעוֹן הַצַּדִּיק. הוּא הָיָה אוֹמֵר: אַל תִּהְיוּ כַּעֲבָדִים הַמְשַׁמְּשִׁין אֶת הָרַב עַל מְנָת לְקַבֵּל פְּרָס, אֶלָּא הֱווּ כַּעֲבָדִים הַמְשַׁמְּשִׁין אֶת הָרַב שֶׁלֹּא עַל מְנָת לְקַבֵּל פְּרָס, וִיהִי מוֹרָא שָׁמַיִם עֲלֵיכֶם.

Antigonus of Sokho received the tradition from Simeon the Tzaddik. He used to say: 'Do not be like servants who serve their master in order to receive a reward. But be like servants who serve the master without the expectation of receiving a reward. And let the fear of Heaven be upon you.'[1]

In the version of this *mishnah* recorded in *Avot de Rabbi Natan*, a significant addition is made at its end: 'In order that your reward may be doubled in the World-to-Come.'[2]

The *mishnah* does not specify from which Simeon the Tzaddik Antigonus received his traditions. There were two Simeons who were called 'the Tzaddik' (see Chapter I), grandfather and grandson. Chronological considerations would indicate that Antigonus studied at the feet of the later Simeon, the grandson; but a case could be made for the earlier Simeon, the grandfather, if we realize that a man who studies an earlier scholar's teachings is considered to be his disciple even if that scholar lived much earlier and died before the disciple was born. It is interesting to note that Antigonus was the first head of the Sanhedrin who was not a *Kohen Gadol*, a High Priest, or even a *Kohen* at all[3].

Our *mishnah* records the only statement by Antigonus found in Talmudic literature. This is surprising. Surely the head of the

Sanhedrin must have offered many religious and philosophical dicta. It must however be remembered that the teachings of the early *tannaim* were delivered orally and many of their sayings were forgotten in the course of the generations before they could be committed to writing. It is also possible that some of his teachings did survive, but anonymously, and were later repeated by other sages and recorded in their name[4].

Be that as it may, the one dictum of Antigonus that has reached us, was taught in a crucial period in Jewish history. Antigonus was, in effect, teaching the correct discipline in serving God. Do good and observe the *mitzvot* of the Torah without thinking of receiving a reward of any kind.

Reward for good deeds is, however, mentioned in the Torah. In Deuteronomy (11:13), in the section which constitutes the second paragraph of the *Keriat Shema*, the Jew's declaration of faith we read: 'And it will be if you obey My commandments which I give you on this day... I will give rain on your land in its season...' Similarly Leviticus (26:3-4) tells us: 'if you walk in My statutes and keep My commandments... I will give your rains in their due season...However, these verses do not contradict Antigonus' teaching. Firstly, the Biblical promises of reward are directed to the People of Israel as a whole; i.e., when all Israel together fulfil the demands of the Torah they will merit their reward. No reward is promised to the individual who observes the *mitzvot* no matter how devout he be. The individual's reward will be given in the real world - the World-to-Come. Secondly, Antigonus did not say that no reward is given for good deeds - he merely said, 'Do not serve God *on condition* that you receive a reward.'

Antigonus' teaching was not correctly understood by two of his students, Zadok and Boethus, and their misinterpretation, together with a number of other factors, tragically led to great conflict and confusion in Jewish national and religious life and created a chasm that lasted for generations.

The two students challenged Antigonus' tradition. If there is no reward for the good that one does on earth, why do good? Is it fair to expect a man to labor for his master and then be denied payment for his work?[5] As to reward in the World-to-Come, where is such a concept mentioned in the Torah? Indeed, they argued, the Torah does not promise any World-to-Come or resurrection of the dead with the coming of the Messiah. As a result of this line of thought, Zadok and Boethus arrived at the conclusion that a man should enjoy all the happiness he can, in whatever form or manner, while he is on this earth. Theirs was a hedonistic philosophy based on the assumption that you should 'eat and drink today, for tomorrow you die.'

Out of this philosophy, two religious sects developed: the Sadducees (Hebrew *Zedukim*, derived from the name Zadok) and the Boethusians. These sects accepted only those laws and ideas which are written explicitly in the Torah. They totally rejected the *Torah she-b'al Peh*, the traditions of Torah interpretation transmitted orally from generation to generation[6].

The sects' adherents came mostly from the upper classes such as merchants. A comparatively large number of *kohanim* identified with these heretical teachings (Zadok was apparently a priest) which, not surprisingly, also attracted a lot of the youth. In the course of time, the Boethusian sect disappeared but the Sadducees played an important - albeit negative-role in later Jewish history.

Extremes breed extremes and the appearance of these heretical sects led to the birth of another sect whose religious philosophy was diametrically opposed to theirs. This was the Essenes who separated themselves form the general Jewish community and created their own with extremely strict rules and regulations. The Essenes preached asceticism and awaited the imminent arrival of the Messiah[7]. Because of their way of life and the limited number of adherents the sect attracted, the Essenes disappeared from the stage of Jewish history very quickly, but they did leave us an 'inheritance' - the Dead Sea Scrolls[8].

Between these two extremes - one preaching hedonism and the other asceticism - stood those who came to be known as Pharisees, whose religious philosophy and practices followed the *mitzvot* of the Torah as interpreted and amplified by the *Torah she-b'al Peh*, the Oral Law, which they believed was a faithful presentation of the traditions handed down by Moses from Sinai. This group is the mainstream of Judaism until this day.

Hellenism, the legacy of Alexander the Great (See Chapter I), began to play a significant role in Jewish life in this period. Greek names, such as Alexander, Antigonus, Theodosius, Alchimes and Jason, became common and even the name of the supreme rabbinical court which had been known as 'The Great Assembly'[9] was changed to Sanhedria (or Sanhedrin) a word of Greek origin. Among certain circles, the Greek way of life, language, customs, ceremonies, art and philosophy became 'the spirit of the day' not only in Eretz Israel but in all the countries of the Middle East that Alexander the Great had conquered. Greek colonists spread throughout the whole region and their settlements had great influence on the local population. In Eretz Israel's southern neighbor, Egypt, Greek became the lingua franca, first of the aristocracy and then of the general population. Ptolemy Philadelphius, King of Egypt, invited 70 Jewish sages to translate the Bible into Greek (the Septuagint) and while Rabban Simeon ben Gamliel states that 'the books of the Scriptures may only be translated into Greek (and not into any other language),'[10] in Tractate Soferim we are told that the day on which the Bible was translated into Greek 'was as hard for Israel as the day on which the Golden Calf was made, because the Torah cannot be accurately translated into any language.'[11]

Miraculously, all the sages translated the difficult and theologically delicate sections identically, without prior consultation. An example of this is the very first verse (Genesis 1:1) which in our English version reads: 'In the beginning, God created heaven and earth...' which they all translated: 'God, in the beginning created...' Another example is: 'And God said, 'let us make man...' (Genesis 1:26) which they rendered into Greek as 'And God said, 'I will make man...' They also translated the verse:'And God finished His work on the seventh day...' (Genesis 2:2) as 'And God concluded on the sixth day...'

However, notwithstanding this miracle, the significance of the text was altered and thus its sanctity was impaired. The word 'Torah' itself was translated as 'Law' a term which implies that it is man-made and can thus be abrogated or changed by man. The word Torah has a much wider and deeper meaning than Law.

Hellenism not only led to the adoption of the Greek language; it brought with it the pagan customs and ceremonies which are so alien to Judaism. It was not long before the Jews of Alexandria, the most important Hellenistic center in Egypt, as well as those in many other communities, began to participate in Greek festivals held in honor of their pantheon of gods. Even the festivals dedicated to Bacchus, the god of wine, which turned into orgies lasting several days, were attended by Jews[12].

In Eretz Israel, the opposition to change and the resistance to Hellenism were at first very strong. But gradually, the Jews of the Holy Land came under the influence of their neighbors, particularly Egypt, with which there was constant communication and contact, and Greek customs began to infiltrate Jewish society.

The Sadducees accepted Hellenism enthusiastically. This was particularly true of the upper social classes who tried to copy the Greek social patterns. However, even they realized that they were in fact implanting foreign ways into Jewish society and attempted to cover up their activities by giving them a 'Jewish taste,' such as the distribution of charity at their Greek-style banquets[13].

Another activity the Hellenists introduced was exceedingly dangerous. This was the institution of Greek athletic games. The Greeks saw these games as a way of uniting the various peoples they had conquered. The games were held in honor of one of the gods, and for the duration of the game a truce was in force between any participating states that might be at war. The present Olympic Games are a modern adaptation of the most famous of the ancient games. In the games, the athletes participated in the nude for two reasons. Firstly, it was an expression of the Greeks' adoration for the human body and secondly it ensured that nobody could smuggle a weapon into the stadium under his cloak.

When the Hellenists started to hold athletic games in Jerusalem, the Jewish participants were often ridiculed because they were circumcised. Because Hellenism was fashionable, many parents did not have their children circumcised to spare them future embarrassment[14] and some aspiring athletes even went so far as to undergo painful surgical operations to have a foreskin grafted[15].

It seems that some aspects of these pagan games were too extreme even for the Hellenists. On one occasion a contingent of Jewish athletes were sent to Tyre to take part in the games and Jason the High Priest, who was a Hellenist, sent money with them to be used for sacrifices to the god Hercules, in whose honor the games were being held. Although the Jewish contestants were Hellenists, they refused to contribute the money for pagan sacrifices because that would label them as idolators. Instead they donated the money to King Antiochus who was outfitting a fleet at Tyre at that time.[16]

The ordinary loyal Jew in Eretz Israel must have been very perplexed by what was happening in the country. The Sadducees, going in the way of Hellenism, were trampling underfoot all that was sacred to the Jews, yet no punishment was meted out from Heaven. It was as though the Almighty was not displeased by what they were doing!

At the same time, no reward was being enjoyed by the Pharisees for their loyalty to Judaism or by the Essenes who were leading an even stricter way of life.

This then was the background of Antigonus' teaching. In the service of God, you should not be concerned about your reward nor should you be discouraged by the fact that the wicked are not punished. Reward and punishment are reserved for the World-to-Come! Let the fear of Heaven ever be upon you.

Antigonus' dictum has another important implication. However pious and devout a person may be, he must never think that a 'little *averah*', a minor transgression, does not count! He must never argue that since he has been observant all his life, it does not matter if now and then he breaks a rule, On the contrary! The more pious a person is, the greater must be his care not to transgress even what may seem to be an unimportant *mitzvah*. This matter has been compared to a shirt - the cleaner a shirt is, the more even the tiniest stain shows up.

At the beginning of this chapter, we suggested that reward on this earth can only be expected if *all* Israel will observe the commandments. This idea is beautifully expressed in the Talmud: 'Rabbi Johanan said in the name of Rabbi Simeon bar Yohai: If Israel were to observe two Sabbaths according to the laws thereof, they would be redeemed at once.'[17]

Thus, we can interpret Antigonus' ending to his one and only *mishnah*:'And let the fear of Heaven be upon upon you' in the following manner: 'And all the nations of the earth will see that the name of God is called on you (because you, Israel, keep the Torah) and they will fear you' (Deuteronomy 28:10). The fear of Heaven will descend upon the nations.

So may it come to pass!

NOTES

1. *Avot* 1:3
2. *Avot de Rabbi Natan* 5
3. Isaac H. Weiss, *Dor Dor ve-Dorshav,* Ch. 11, p.85
4. *Berakhot 43b:* Rav Zutra bar Tobiah said in the name of Rav etc.
5. *Avot D'Rabbi Natan* 5
6. Josephus, *Antiquities* 18:1:14; *Sanhedrin* 90a/b
7. *Enziklopediah Talmudit:* Hellenism
8. *Ibid,* Dead Sea Scrolls
9. *Avot* 1:2
10. *Megillah* 9b
11. *Soferim* 1:7
12. Graetz, *History of the Jews* (English edition), vol.1, Ch. 21
13. *Ibid,* p.428
14. Isaac H. Weiss, *Dor Dor ve-Dorshav,* vol. 1, p.97
15. Graetz, *History of the Jews* (English edition), vol. 1, p. 445-6
16. *Ibid,* p. 446
17. *Shabbat* 118b

Yose ben Yoezer of Zeredah

יוֹסֵי בֶּן יוֹעֶזֶר אִישׁ צְרֵדָה, וְיוֹסֵי בֶּן יוֹחָנָן אִישׁ יְרוּשָׁלַיִם קִבְּלוּ
מֵהֶם. יוֹסֵי בֶּן יוֹעֶזֶר אִישׁ צְרֵדָה אוֹמֵר: יְהִי בֵיתְךָ בֵּית וַעַד
לַחֲכָמִים, וֶהֱוֵי מִתְאַבֵּק בַּעֲפַר רַגְלֵיהֶם, וֶהֱוֵי שׁוֹתֶה בַצָּמָא אֶת
דִּבְרֵיהֶם.

*Yose ben Yoezer of Zeredah and Yose ben Johanan of
Jerusalem received the tradition from them. Yose ben
Yoezer of Zeredah said: Let your home be a meeting place
for the wise, sit in the dust of their feet and drink their words
with thirst.*[1]

An immediate question arises: From whom did Yose ben
Yoezer and Yose ben Johanan receive the tradition? The
mishnah states 'from them' but in the previous *mishnah* only
Antigonus of Sokho is mentioned[2]. It is possible that the
reference is to Antigonus and Simeon the Tzaddik, the
grandson (See Chapter 2). This would mean that both
Antigonus and the two Yoses were the second Simeon's
disciples. When the latter died, Antigonus was elevated to the
leadership and when he, in his turn, died, the two Yoses took
over the leadership of the Sanhedrin.

It can also be assumed that Antigonus was so well versed in
the first Simeon the Tzaddik's teachings, that when he taught
he transmitted both his own thoughts and those of his
predecessor.

The Meiri, in his remarks on our *mishnah*, states that
although only Antigonus is mentioned by name, the intention
is to the whole Sanhedrin of which Antigonus was the head.

The Sanhedrin also constituted a *yeshivah* and the two Yoses, being the most brilliant of the students, became the religious leaders of the nation on the death of Antigonus. Thus, the 'them'of the *mishnah* refers to the members of the Sanhedrin.

Yose ben Yoezer and Yose ben Johanan were the first of the five *Zugot* (Pairs) of sages who headed the Sanhedrin, as is indicated in Avot.[3] In each case, the first sage mentioned was the *Nasi*, President, of the Sanhedrin, and the second was *Av Bet Din*, the operative head of the court.

Yose ben Yoezer and Yose ben Johanan are also described as *Eshkolot* (literally, Clusters), which is explained as a contraction of *Ish She-ha-kol Bo*, a man who contains all (knowledge)[4]. Rabbi Judah said in the name of Samuel: 'All the *Eshkolot* who arose in Israel from the days of Moses until Yose ben Yoezer and Yose ben Johanan studied Torah like Moses; from then on, they did not study Torah like Moses.' The *Gemara* continues: 'From the days of Moses until the death of the two Yoses there was no *dofi* (taint) in any of the *Eshkolot*, but after their death there was.'[5] In another *mishnah* we are told that 'with the death of Yose ben Yoezer and Yose ben Johanan the *Eshkolot* ceased.'[6]

From these sources it is clear that the later rabbis held the two Yoses in very great esteem and that, in some sense, they marked a water-shed in Jewish history. The *Gemara* itself, however, questions the comparison to Moses.[7] We know that in the period of mourning for Moses no less than 3,000 laws were forgotten and a majority vote was required to decide the *Halakhah* in those cases. Thus, Moses knew at least 3,000 more laws than did the two Yoses and how can their knowledge be compared to his? The answer is that what was forgotten was forgotten,but with regards to what was not forgotten, the two Yoses knew the material as well as Moses.

From the time of the Return to Zion under Ezra and Nehemiah, the religious and political leadership of Israel had been invested in one man, the *Kohen Gadol*, the High Priest.[8]

From the time of Antigonus, however, the situation changed. The *Kohen Gadol* remained the political head of the country, but the religious leadership passed into the hands of the *Nasi* of the Sanhedrin. Antigonus, who filled the latter position, was not even a *kohen* and although Yose ben Yoezer was and is described as 'the most pious scion the priesthood,'[9] he was not *Kohen Gadol* because in his time the High-Priesthood was a political appointment which was made by the foreign governor of the country. Changes of incumbents were so frequent that we do not know the names of many of the High Priests[10] and, indeed, simony was commonly practiced with regard to this, the highest office in Israel.

The two Yoses lived in an extremely turbulent period in Jewish history. We have already seen how various sects developed and how Hellenism began to influence Jewish life. The period was also one of military struggle between Egypt and Syria. Eretz Israel, situated as it was between these two major powers, suffered greatly. Antiochus, the Syrian emperor, prohibited the study of Torah and even the possession of a Hebrew volume was a capital offence.[11] Nevertheless, Yose ben Yoezer exhorted the people: 'Let your home be a meeting place for the wise,' and he was not referring to Greek philosophers.

Many people were afraid to be seen in the company of a rabbi lest they be suspected of breaking the draconian laws. Others, in order to curry favor in the eyes of the Hellenistic authorities, invited Greeks into their homes to demonstrate that they were making every effort to comply with the Emperor's desire to Hellenize the Jewish people. This was especially true of the Sadducees and the aristocrats who exhibited great reverence for the pearls of Hellenistic wisdom which their guests would cast before them. This then was the social and political background of Yose's plea to the Jews: Invite only the rabbinic sages into your home! Drink only their words with thirst.

The situation in Eretz Israel was so bad that many Jews

emigrated so as to be able to study Torah and practice Judaism without fear. No wonder then, that Yose ben Yoezer declared that foreign lands were 'spiritually impure', and that any person who went out of Eretz Israel would have to undergo the process of purification to be able to enter the Temple precincts.[12] This was undoubtedly an effort to stem the tide of emigration. At the same time, glass utensils manufactured outside Eretz Israel were declared impure and given the status of earthenware vessels. This was to protect the local craftsmen against foreign competition and encourage local industry.

From the above it might seem that Yose ben Yoezer tended towards strictness in his rulings, yet he was known as 'Yose the Permitter' because of three important decisions.[13] He permitted a certain type of locust to be eaten; he ruled that the blood and water which flowed from the place of slaughter in the Temple did not cause impurity; and he decided that a person who came into contact with a corpse and so became unclean (Numbers 19:16) did not defile other persons with whom he came into contact.

This last ruling had important practical consequences. Yose ben Yoezer lived at the time of the Maccabean wars against Syria and the Hellenists, the success of which we celebrate on Hanukkah. Many extremely pious men, including members of the Essene sect, were reluctant to take part in the struggle because of their concern about spiritual purity. It was important to them to stay spiritually pure and they were apprehensive lest they come into contact with combat soldiers who had touched a corpse. The third of Yose's rulings described above enabled such people to join the struggle for Jewish independence.

Yose ben Yoezer and Yose ben Johanan governed the spiritual life of Israel in complete harmony except for one severe disagreement. This was with regard to whether the 'laying of hands' ceremony on an animal to be sacrificed could be performed on a festival.[14] Yose ben Yoezer claimed that the ceremony was not an intrinsic part of the preparation of the animal for human consumption and constituted an act of labor. Thus it was forbidden on a festival, since only those acts of labor which prepare the animal for consumption are allowed.Yose ben Johanan disagreed and argued that the 'laying of hands' ceremony was an integral part of the process leading to the animal's sacrifice which permitted it to be eaten and thus could be performed on a festival. According to his opinion, this is the law even with regard to the *olot* sacrifices which are burned on the altar and not eaten by human beings - the consumption of the Almighty is no less significant than that of human beings. It is extremely interesting that this point was the issue between the members of the four subsequent *Zugot* and was finally decided by Hillel[15] against the opinion of Shammai; (see Chapter 7). This difference of opinion between the two Yoses is described in the Talmud as the first *mahloket,* halakhic difference of opinion, in rabbinic history.

In one place in the Talmud it is suggested that Yose ben Yoezer did not conduct himself in a proper manner.[16] It is recorded that he had a 'loft' (according to Tosafot, a large vessel for storing wine or oil) of gold coins and because his son did not conduct himself in a manner befitting his family status, he disinherited him and gave the money to the Temple instead. His son subsequently married and when his wife gave birth he bought a large fish, apparently for the banquet to celebrate the event. When the fish was opened, a very valuable precious stone was discovered. Yose's son took the stone to the Temple treasurer for valuation. The stone was exceedingly beautiful and the Temple treasurer told Yose's son that it was worth thirteen 'lofts' of gold coins and that he would have wanted to buy it for the Temple but that the Temple treasury had only seven 'lofts' at that time. Yose's son accepted the seven 'lofts' and gave the stone to the Temple. This led some of the rabbis to say that whereas Yose had given only one 'loft' to the Temple, his son had given six - not a very favorable comment as far as

Yose was concerned. Other rabbis, however, saw it differently. Yose had given the Temple one 'loft' of gold; his son had taken seven.

Yose ben Yoezer met a tragic end. The *midrash*[17] relates that he was sentenced to death by crucifixion, presumably for teaching Torah. As he was carrying the cross to the place of crucifixion, he was met by his nephew, Jakim, also known as Alcimus, who was a Hellenist and had been appointed High Priest. Although it was Shabbat, Alcimus was riding a horse. The *midrash* records the following conversation:

Alcimus:' Uncle, become a Hellenist! Look at me. I am riding a horse and soon you will be riding that beam you are carrying.'

Yose: 'Never! If your's is the reward for those who anger Him, how much greater will be the reward of those who do His will.'

Alcimus: 'Has anybody done His will more than you?'

Yose: 'If this is the punishment of those who do His will, how much greater will be that of those who anger Him!'

These words pierced Alcimus to the quick and he committed suicide in a most unique manner. According to the Torah there are four methods of execution inflicted by the *Bet Din*: stoning; burning; decapitation by sword; and strangulation. Alcimus knew that execution by the *Ben Din* brings forgiveness for transgression and so he decided to commit suicide by all four methods of execution. He built a pyre at the center of which was a sword and above which were stones. He lit the pyre and hanged himself over it. The flames burnt through the rope and he fell onto the sword and the stones fell on him. The *midrash* adds that Yose, hanging on the cross but still alive, saw Alcimus ascending to heaven and exclaimed 'My nephew is getting there before me!'

According to Josephus,[18] Alcimus met his death when he tried to dismantle the walls around the Temple. As he was about to start, he dropped dead.

Yose, the *Eshkol* who studied Torah like Moses and in whom there was no taint, died on the cross but we can well imagine him saying to the weeping Jews who accompanied him on his last journey: 'Do not grieve for me and be not discouraged! Hellenism will disappear but Judaism will live if only you follow my teachings. Open your homes to the sages, sit at their feet and drink their words of Torah with thirst.'

All who know the story of Hanukkah know how true his words were. Hellenism did disappear and we, today, study the words of Yose ben Yoezer of Zeredah.

NOTES

1. *Avot* 1:4
2. *Ibid*, 1:3
3. *Ibid*, 1:4,6,8,10,12
4. *Temurah* 15b
5. *Ibid*
6. *Sotah* 47a
7. *Temurah* 15b
8. *Avot* 1:2
9. *Hagigah* 20a
10. Yoma 71b
11. Josephus, *Antiquities* 12:5:4
12. *Shabbat* 14b
13. *Avodah Zarah* 37a
14. *Hagigah* 16a/b
15. *TJ Hagigah* 2:3
16. *Bava Batra* 133b; but see the conclusion there.
17. *Midrash Rabbah*, Genesis 65:22
18. Josephus, *Antiquities* 12:10:6

Yose ben Johanan of Jerusalem

יוֹסֵי בֶּן יוֹחָנָן אִישׁ יְרוּשָׁלַיִם אוֹמֵר: יְהִי בֵיתְךָ פָּתוּחַ לִרְוָחָה,
וְיִהְיוּ עֲנִיִּים בְּנֵי בֵיתֶךָ, וְאַל תַּרְבֶּה שִׂיחָה עִם הָאִשָּׁה, בְּאִשְׁתּוֹ
אָמְרוּ, קַל וָחֹמֶר בְּאֵשֶׁת חֲבֵרוֹ. מִכָּאן אָמְרוּ חֲכָמִים: כָּל הַמַּרְבֶּה
שִׂיחָה עִם הָאִשָּׁה גּוֹרֵם רָעָה לְעַצְמוֹ וּבוֹטֵל מִדִּבְרֵי תוֹרָה וְסוֹפוֹ
יוֹרֵשׁ גֵּיהִנָּם.

> *Yose ben Johanan of Jerusalem said: 'Let your home be open*
> *wide and let the poor be members of your household; and do*
> *not talk a lot with the woman.' The intention here is to your*
> *own wife; how much more so does the rule apply to*
> *somebody else's wife! On the basis of the dictum the sages*
> *said: 'Whoever engages in much gossip with women brings*
> *harm to himself, neglects the study of Torah, and will, in the*
> *end, go to Gehinom.'*[1]

The simple meaning of the first part of our *mishnah* is: Make
your home into a place of hospitality where a poor man or a
wayfarer feels welcome; where he is fed and where he can rest
and be comfortable.

In the preceding *mishnah*, Yose ben Yoezer, (Yose ben
Johanan's colleague) had exhorted the reader to make his
home into a gathering place for the wise, which would seem to
exclude the unlearned. Our *tanna* is concerned for the poor and
he speaks of the *mitzvah* of hospitality to all people, regardless
of their learning.

With our *mishnah*, the teaching of Simeon the Tzaddik, 'The
world is based on three principles: *Torah; Avodah; Gemilut
Hasadim*,'[2] has now been elaborated upon. Antigonus of

Sokho has talked of *Avodah*, service to God;[3] Yose ben Yoezer has described one aspect of *Torah*;[4] and Yose ben Johanan has now explained what *Gemilut Hasadim* is.

In fact, the ideal which Yose ben Johanan demands from every Jew in his practice of *Gemilut Hasadim* was set by the patriarch, Abraham. The *midrash* quotes Rabbi Abbahu as saying: 'The tent of our father Abraham was open at both ends so that from whichever direction a wayfarer came, Abraham would run to greet him and invite him into the tent. He would have him wash his feet(i.e., refresh himself), rest and eat something before going on his way.'[5]

Avot D'Rabbi Natan[6] tells us that Job emulated Abraham and praised him highly for his hospitality. Job's home had doors on all four sides so that from whichever direction a visitor or poor man approached he would be able to enter. The fact that he did not have to look for the entrance reduced any embarrassment he might have felt and made him realize that he really was welcome. There was no special entrance for the poor; Job's home did not have a servant's entrance, a tradesman's entrance or a pauper's entrance. When poor people met, they spoke of Job with high regard and Job himself referred to his hospitality in his appeal to the Almighty: Was there a poor man, an orphan or a widow who came to me that I did not feed and clothe? (a paraphrase of Job 31:17-20).

There was, however, a major difference between Abraham's practice of hospitality and Job's. The latter waited for the poor and needy to come to him, whereas Abraham would seek them out and when he saw wayfarers from a distance he would take the initiative and run to greet them and invite them in, no matter who they were. Abraham, as is clear from the story of the three disguised angels(Genesis 18), used to escort his guests on their way to make sure that they did not get lost. Abraham acted *lifnim mi-shurat ha-din*, above and beyond the requirements of the law.

Later in history, Rabbi Jehudah the Nasi, the redactor of the

Mishnah, was reminded of Yose ben Johanan's dictum when, in a time of drought, he opened his storehouses but stipulated that only the learned could benefit from his generosity. When one scholar pointed out that Almighty God feeds even animals Rabbi Judah realized his mistake and supplied all the needy regardless of their learning (see Chapter 15).[7]

It would seem that Yose ben Johanan's dictum was followed only by his fellow Pharisees. According to *Avot D'Rabbi Natan,*[8] the Sadducees used to eat off gold and silver vessels. How could a poor man be invited to join a table so richly equipped? He would surely feel envious and uncomfortable and would not enjoy the food he was eating. Furthermore, as we have seen in Chapter 3, the Hellenists and the Sadducees were only interested in practicing hospitality for their own benefit. They invited guests who could enhance their own prestige and who would reciprocate and improve their social standing. It may well be that Yose's words were, in effect, a rebuke aimed at such people to tell them that their behavior did not constitute true hospitality.

Similarly, the Essenes were at fault in their practice of hospitality. They were extremely strict in their observance of ritual purity and would not mingle with the poor who might be ritually unclean and 'contaminate' their hosts and the food. Some Essenes were so pious that they did not marry because they were afraid their wives would not be able to maintain the extreme standard of ritual purity the sect required. The Pharisees were also concerned about ritual purity, but they realized that the *mitzvah* of feeding the hungry and clothing the naked is so important that they extended themselves in order to perform it. According to the *midrash*, Abraham even extended his hospitality to pagans; he had them wash their feet so as not to bring the dust of the ways, which they worshipped, into his home.

In the final analysis, the *mitzvah* of *Hakhnassat Orchim* benefits the one who practices it. The poor man leaves his benefactor with a blessing in his heart and on his lips, as we learn: 'Everyone who was a guest in Abraham's home prayed, 'May the Almighty bless you for your kindness!' and the prayers of the poor, because they are made sincerely, are heard.

The *Mishna* continues: "and do not talk a great deal with the woman." In *Avot D'Rabbi Natan*[8] the same *Mishna* ends at this point. The redactor of our *Mishna* then adds the admonishment "even with your own wife, how much more so with a strange woman."

To this our Sages add, "whoever engages in much gossip merits purgatory."

Clearly, a man cannot invite guests to his home without telling his wife and ensuring that the guests will be made welcome. Abraham knew that his wife, Sarah, was a kindred spirit. On the verse: 'And Abram took Sarai his wife...and all the souls that they had made...'(Genesis 12:5), the *midrash*[9] comments: 'Rabbi Hunna said, 'Abraham used to convert the men (to the service of God) and Sarah used to convert the women.' Indeed, on the verse (*ibid*,18:6): 'And he (Abraham) said (to Sarah), 'Hurry! Take three measures of *kemah solet* (fine flour), knead them and make cakes (for the guests).' The *midrash* explains that Abraham told her to use ordinary flour but Sarah insisted on making the cakes from the better and more expensive fine flour.

The Talmud and the *midrashim* are full of dicta about how a man is to treat his wife. The Jewish respect for the lady-of-the-house started as far back as Abraham when God told him, 'All that Sarah says to you, listen to her!'(Genesis 21:12). According to the Talmud,[10] the verse, 'And you shall know that your tent (home) will be in peace' (Job 5:24), applies to the man 'who loves his wife as himself and honors her more than himself.' In another passage in the Talmud[11] we find three extremely sensitive insights into the relationship between husband and wife. Rav said: 'One should be heedful of wronging one's wife; because a woman is quick to tears, she is easily hurt.' In the context of the discussion there, Rav Papa quoted a widespread folk-saying, 'If your wife is short, bend down to listen to her whisperings,' and Rabbi Hilbo summed up generally accepted rabbinic attitude with, 'A man must be careful with regard to the honor due to his wife - for blessings rest in a man's house only on account of his wife.' Yet our *mishnah* seems to imply that one should not spend time talking to a woman, even one's own wife.

To understand the *mishnah* correctly we must look at the Hebrew term it employs. The word for talk in our mishnah is *sihah*, which implies an element of gossip. Yose ben Johanan was not restricting serious conversation but was referring to gossip, because gossip means speaking ill of others. People love to gossip and, indeed, gossip is considered to be one of the most widespread of sins. But it is also one of the most grievous! According to the rabbis, 'For three sins a man is punished in this world and is denied life in the World-to-Come: idolatry, sexual immorality, and bloodshed. And *lashon ha-ra* (evil tongue, gossip), is as grievous as all of them!' Furthermore, Rabbi Johanan ruled that 'he who speaks *lashon ha-ra* is as though he denies the existence of God!'[12] These statements are not just moral exhortations but were later codified into law by Maimonides. *Lashon ha-ra* destroys three people: the one who speaks it, the one who listens to it, and the one about whom it is spoken. Therefore the speaker deserves Gehinom, hell, for destroying two other people!

The rise of Hellenism in Israel was not just a question of an alien philosophy. It had brought with it a totally strange way of life which included wild parties and lewd entertainment which led to immorality. This was against all that was holy for the Jews. The Jewish ideal was a chaste, humble life with man directing his talents and energies to higher deeds. The extravagant hedonism and immorality which accompanied the Greeks wherever they went were abhorrent to the rabbis and the majority of Jews. During this period there was a sharp increase in prostitution to the extent the the Talmud[13] advises scholars not to talk even to their wives, daughters or sisters in public because the spectators may not know of the relationship and suspect immoral behavior. In Chapter 19 we read of the great sage, Rabbi Simeon bar Yohai, who was sentenced to death because he spoke out against the Romans for facilitation immorality.[14] The situation became so vile that the Talmud[15] sadly reports: 'When cases of adultery multiplied, they stopped administrating the bitter waters to a woman whose husband suspected her of adultery (Numbers 5:11-28).' This was because the waters were effective only when adultery was the exception and not the norm.

The rabbis, in their opposition to the new philosophies espoused by the Hellenists and the Saducees, were well aware that the avowals of humanism and dignity were nothing more than excuses for debauchery and immorality which could very well destroy the moral fabric of the Jewish people. The danger was so great that the sages went to extreme lengths in their attempt to stem the spread of the disease. Yose ben Johanan was saying that what starts in what may appear to be innocent conversation can lead to over-familiarity which, in turn, breeds contempt for learning and steals time from it. The final result can be a descent into immorality and Gehinom.

NOTES

1. *Avot* 1:5
2. *Avot* 1:2
3. *Avot* 1:3
4. *Avot* 1:4
5. *Midrash Rabbah,* Genesis 48:9
6. *Avot D'Rabbi Natan*, 21a
7. *Bava Batra 8a*
8. *Avot D'Rabbi Natan*, chapter 7-21a
9. *Midrash Rabbah*, Genesis 39:14
10. *Yevamot* 62b
11. *Bava Metzia* 59a
12. *Arakhim* 15a
13. *Berakhot* 43b
14. *Shabbat* 33b
15. *Sotah* 47b

Simeon ben Shatah

שִׁמְעוֹן בֶּן שָׁטַח אוֹמֵר: הֱוֵי מַרְבֶּה לַחֲקֹר אֶת הָעֵדִים, וֶהֱוֵי זָהִיר בִּדְבָרֶיךְ שֶׁמָּא מִתּוֹכָם יִלְמְדוּ לְשַׁקֵּר.

Simeon ben Shatach states: Examine the witnesses thoroughly but be careful with your words, lest through them they learn to falsify.[1]

This directive, of one of the greatest sages, is aimed primarily at the judges who must interrogate witnesses intensively to arrive at the truth. They must, however, take great care in formulating their questions otherwise there is a danger that the witnesses will be "led" to give the answers they think the judges expect. One can also understand the directive as being relevant to ordinary people too. Never accept what you hear at its face value; gossip, *lashon ha-ra* - "the evil tongue", has, as they say, a beard each one who repeats it adds just "a hair" and the story you hear may very well be entirely different from what actually happened.

Simeon ben Shatach was a distinguished judge and indeed played a major role in developing the rabbinic system of justice. It is recorded[2] that he condemned 80 witches to death by hanging on one day. The law is that a court can not hold two capital trials on one day. This is to ensure that each case receives thorough consideration and that every effort is made to find some reason to acquit the accused. Furthermore, although there is a minority opinion - Rabbi Eliezer's - that women can be hanged, the majority ruling is that only men can be hung and not women. Rashi explains Simeon's action by saying that sorcery was rife at that time as is clear from the fact that in one town, Ashkelon, there were as many as 80 witches and that the step was extra-judicial because of the state of emergency. The Jerusalem Talmud tells the story of the witches and comments briefly: "Although two cases can not be tried on one day, the hour demanded it."

Judah ben Tabbai, Simeon ben Shatach's closest associate, was also involved in a rare judicial incident in which he condemned a man to death as an emergency measure because "the hour demanded it."[3] The law is that false witnesses, *edim zomemim,* are given the same punishment that they intended to inflict on their victim (Deuteronomy 19:19). This is interpreted to mean that they receive that punishment only if it had *not* been carried out on the accused; if, however, the sentence on the accused had already been carried out before the witnesses were discovered to be false, they do not receive the same punishment because their conspiracy can no longer be defined as "intent;" it has already become a fact. The Sadducee sect did not accept this rabbinic interpretation and insisted that the opposite was the law: the witnesses were to be executed only if their victim had already been executed.[3] Judah ben Tabbai and Simeon ben Shatach lived in a period of intense struggle between the Sadducees and the Pharisees, as the normative rabbinic stream is generally known, and Judah ben Tabbai condemned a false witness to death to demonstrate that the rabbinic interpretation was correct.[3] However, in his zeal to make his point against the Sadducees, Judah overlooked another law. False witnesses are to be punished only if both of them are found to be false; if only one is found to be false he can not be punished.

Simeon ben Shatach brought Judah's mistake to his attention in no uncertain fashion and Judah undertook never to sit in judgement without Simeon who could check his decisions. For the rest of his life, Judah visited the executed witness' grave to beg forgiveness for his error.[3]

The laws of testimony are extremely strict and are aimed at

eliminating any possibility of judicial mistakes. In many cases the court is powerless to act even if it "knows" the truth because the necessary testimony is absent. Simeon himself was once faced with an extreme example of this and said: "I once saw a man with a sword in his hand chase another into a ruin. I ran after them and the pursuer emerged with his sword dripping blood and the victim writhing. I exclaimed, "Wicked man! You killed him! But I can do nothing for it is written: At the mouth of two witnesses...shall the accused be put to death' (Deuteronomy 17:6)."[4] Circumstantial evidence is not acceptable in Jewish law and evidence of the act must be given by at least two witnesses.

The Talmud is ambivalent in its attitude to Simeon's decision with regards to the witches and states that "Simeon had hot (impulsive) hands."[5] That affair had tragic consequences for Simeon himself. A group of the relatives of the executed witches conspired against Simeon's son and gave evidence that he had committed murder. Justice took its course and Simeon's son was condemned to death. When he was being led out to his execution, the conspirators had a change of heart and confessed that they had given false evidence in order to revenge themselves on Simeon. The latter wanted to cancel the execution but his son reminded him that the law was, that after sentencing, witnesses can not withdraw their testimony and that he, Simeon, if he wanted "to save Israel", i.e. make rabbinic law the norm of the people, must be consequential in his judicial activities and "use me as a door-mat." The law must stand above all other considerations.[5]

In view of these experiences, it is not hard to understand Simeon's exhortation to judges to "examine witnesses thoroughly."

Just as Simeon ben Shatach did not hesitate to admonish his distinguished colleague, Judah ben Tabbai, when the correct dispensation of justice was involved, so too he showed no fear of royalty. Simeon was the brother of Queen Alexandra, the consort of King Alexander Jannai.[6] Once, Jannai's slave killed a man and was ordered to stand trial before the Sanhedrin. The king, as his master and owner, was ordered to stand trial with him.[7] Alexander Jannai appeared in court and sat down. Simeon, as president of the court, ordered him to stand since he was on trial before God but the king stood on his dignity and refused. Simeon turned to the other members of the court and asked their opinion as to what course of action to take. One by one, they lowered their heads out of fear of the king. Most of the court's members at that time were Sadducees whereas Simeon was the leader of the Pharisees. Simeon prophesied that a day would come when their "heads would be lowered" and indeed later many of them were killed in King Alexander Jannai's purges.[8] Because of this incident, it was enacted that a king can neither judge nor be judged and that testimony cannot be accepted against him.[7]

Many of the sages fled to Egypt to escape the king's wrath and others, including Simeon went into hiding.[9] Throughout his reign, Alexander Jannai favored the Sadducees who were more accomodating to the throne than the rabbinic sages, but on his deathbed he advised the queen to rely on the Pharisees because they were not hypocrites.[10] After his death, Alexandra ruled and her brother, Simeon ben Shatach came out of hiding to resume his post. He sent messages to Alexandria in Egypt urging the sages to return to Jerusalem particularly Joshua ben Perahia[11] and Judah ben Tabbai.[12] When the latter returned, Simeon relinquished his position of *Nasi* to him and took the secondary post of *Av Bet Din* until Judah's mistake over the false witness when they exchanged positions.

For the duration of Queen Alexandra's reign, Simeon ben Shatach was the *de facto* ruler of Eretz Israel. The queen bowed to his advice and the country enjoyed several years of peace and prosperity. One of Simeon's major problems was the Sadducean party. This was led by priestly aristocrats who opposed the dissemination of Torah knowledge among the people. They wanted Judaism to be a religion like the other contemperaneous religions in which the Temple priests were the only ones who needed to be educated. Simeon, in the words of the Talmud, brought back the glory of the Torah by establishing a system of public schools for young children.[13] Another area of conflict between the Sadducees and the Pharisees was the interpretation of the Torah. The Sadducees were fundamentalists; they believed that the Torah was not to be interpreted but was to be taken literally. Thus, they rejected the Oral Law and denied that there was a tradition of interpretation handed down from Moses. At one time, Simeon ben Shatach was the only non-Sadducee in the Sanhedrin but later succeeded in replacing the Sadducean judges with rabbinic sages.[14] His method was to ask members of the court for decisions and then demand proof from the Torah. The Sadducees were unable to supply the proof and were replaced by Pharisees.

It was certainly Simeon's preoccupation with the judicial system that led him to stress the importance of examining the witnesses in order to arrive at the truth. Nevertheless, he warns the judges not to "lead" the witnesses into giving false testimony. Judah ben Tabbai spelt this out even more explicitly: "Do not behave as counselors; when the litigants are standing before you, regard them both as wicked, but when they leave, regard them both as innocent when they accept the verdict."[15]

An indication of the prosperity the country enjoyed in Simeon's days, can be found in the Talmud's statement that in his days the grains of wheat grew as large as beans or eggs.[16] Yet it was Simeon ben Shatach who rebuked Honi Ha-Meagel for demanding of the Almighty to cause rain to fall.

It happened that no rain fell during the month of Adar. The people sent to Honi Ha-Meagel (Honi the Circle Maker), a renowned saint, to pray for rain. He drew a circle on the ground around himself and said "I will not move out of this circle until it rains." As he prayed, a light rain began. "No! This is not the rain I pray for!" It began to pour. "No! This is also not what I am praying for! I want rain that will be a blessing and fill the cisterns, springs and wells!" It rained so much that the people had to seek shelter in high places until Honi prayed for the rain to stop. It did.[17]

Simeon ben Shatach sent to Honi: "I should really have you excommunicated for your presumption, but what can I do, you are like a son imploring his Father in Heaven and He listens to you!"[18]   Now, how can the Talmud tell us that wheat grew in such great abundance and then tell us of a drought so severe that Honi Ha-Meagel had to be called in? This contradiction can be reconciled if we consider the two periods in Simeon's life. In the first, the Sadducees were in power and Israel was on the wrong path. God withheld the rain in punishment and it needed Honi's intercession to save the situation. Later, however, when Simeon restored the honor of the Torah, established schools and reconstituted the Sanhedrin, Israel was back on the right way and the rains fell in their season and brought with them their blessings.

As the leader of the nation, Simeon ben Shatach instituted social regulations to improve the people's lives. An outstanding example of this is the *ketubbah,* the marriage agreement. In former times, the bridegroom had to deposit money with the bride's father so that in case of his dying first or divorcing her, she would be safeguarded and have enough to live on. This created a great deal of hardship and the marriage rate declined. To correct this situation, it was decreed that the bridegroom merely promised to make payment in the event of his pre-decease or divorce from the estate. This did not help a great deal since the obligation was unsecured and the bride had no surety. Simeon changed this to a secured committment on the part of the groom by which all his present and future property was mortgaged to honor his obligation. Thus, in those cases where the wife might have to claim her rights and there was nothing in the estate to claim from, she could go back and retrieve anything the husband had sold or disposed of since the marriage.[19] This system exists till this day.

Simeon was equally concerned with the welfare of non-Jews. The Talmud records[20] that Simeon made his livelihood by dealing in flax and actually used to carry it himself. His students, wanting to lighten their teacher's burden, bought him a donkey as a gift. After the purchase they discvovered a precious stone suspended around the donkey's neck and Simeon ordered them to return in to the previous owner, a non-Jew. "You paid for a donkey, not a precious stone." One can imagine the esteem and honor that Judaism gained in the eyes of that gentile. Actions speak louder than words. And Simeon may have taught his disciples more by his deeds than by his lectures, for, as we learn elsewhere in Avot,[21] it is not the lecture that counts but the deed.

In the same vein, Simeon ben Shatach's behavior with King Alexander Jannai left its mark on his two distinguished pupils, Shemayah and Avtalion, who in their day, brought Herod to trial.[22] That incident is fully explained in Chapter VI

Notes

1. *Avot* 1:9
2. *Sanhedrin* 45b/46a; *TJ Sanhedrin* 6:6
3. *Makkot* 5b; *Tj Sanhedrin 6:3 - Pnay Moshe on same.*
4. *Sanhedrin* 37b
5. *TJ Sanhedrin* 6:3
6. *Barakhot* 48a
7. *Sanhedrin* 19a/b
8. *Kiddushin* 66a
9. *Sotah* 47a
10. Josephus, *Antiquities* 13:15:5
11. *Sotah* 47a
12. *TJ Hagigah* 2:2
13. *TJ Ketubbot* 8:11
14. *Megilat Ta'anit* 10
15. *Avot* 1:8
16. *Hullin* 119b; *Ta'anit* 23a
17. *Ta'anit* 23a
18. *Berakhot* 9a; *Ta'anit* 19a
19. *Ketubbot* 82b; *TJ Ketubbot* 8:11
20. *TJ Bava Mezia* 2:5
21. *Avot* 1:17
22. Josephus, *Antiquities* 14:9:4

Shemayah and Avtalyon

שְׁמַעְיָה וְאַבְטַלְיוֹן קִבְּלוּ מֵהֶם. שְׁמַעְיָה אוֹמֵר: אֱהֹב אֶת
הַמְּלָאכָה, וּשְׂנָא אֶת הָרַבָּנוּת, וְאַל תִּתְוַדַּע לָרָשׁוּת.

*Shemayah and Avtalyon received the tradition from them
(Judah ben Tabbai and Simeon ben Shatach). Shemayah
said: Love work; hate lordship; and seek no intimacy with
the ruling power.*[1]

Is this Mishnah to be considered as one dictum or are they three
distinct and separate maxims?

Shemayah offered three pieces of advice that for all their
universal relevance, have their origin in the personal
experience of these two great rabbis. They lived in the 1st
century B.C.E. during what is known as the Herodian period.
The Talmud tells us that: "Descendants of Sennacherib (the
king of Assyria who besieged Jerusalem and desisted because
of a miracle (II Kings 19:35) taught Torah in public. And who
were they? Shemayah and Avtalyon."[2]

Since Shemayah and Avtalyon were members of the
Sanhedrin, the Supreme Court of the Jewish people, they could
not themselves have been proselytes for the law is clear: "All
who may judge in capital cases, may judge in monetary cases;
but not all who may judge in monetary cases may judge in
capital cases, for example, proselytes."[3] And the Sanhedrin
ruled in capital cases. Similarly, the Jerusalem Talmud[4]
teaches that if the panel of judges included one who was not
eligible to sit in judgement, such as a proselyte, the decision of
that court is null and void.

From this it is clear that Shemayah and Avtalyon must have been descendants of converts to Judaism and this fact is extremely important for understanding their behavior as we shall see. Indeed even their names may have indicated their origins. Shemayah means "He heard (the voice of) God" and perhaps refers to the "call" to convert that his proselyte ancestor heard. While Avtalyon means "The father of small children," and may signify the new spiritual commitment of future generations of his family. Obadiah of Bertinoro, one of the most important commentators on the Mishnah, explains the latter's name as indicating that he, as president of the Sanhedrin, was the legal guardian of small children and orphans.[5]

Shemayah and Avtalyon were the two most important rabbis of their generation and were very sensitive regarding their families' non-Jewish origins.

The Rambam (Maimonides) as well as many other commentators, state that Shemayah and Avtalyon were themselves the converts. They answer the question raised both in the Babylonian and in the Jerusalem Talmud with various responsa.

We find in every generation - emergencies arose that made it necessary to enact "special laws" that seemed to be contrary to the Halacha. The Sages based their ruling on the sentence, "It is time for Thee,Oh Lord, to work, for they have made void Thy law." (Psalm 119:126)

Since Shemayah and Avtalyon were the most learned Sages of their day, the rule that converts are not permitted to sit in certain cases of judgment was set aside. They became the exception to the rule.

Harav Hagaon Rabbi J.D. Soloveitchik, in one of his lectures, stated that from all indications, they themselves were the converts but, that they probably absented themselves from cases where, if they were present and had to give a ruling, the rulings would be unacceptable since they were converts. Others are of the opinion that since they were the heads of the Sanhedrin they were eligible to participate in *all* cases.

On one occasion, they ruled that a freed bond-woman (who has the status of a proselyte) who was suspected of infidelity by her husband, had to undergo the *sotah* process in which the suspected woman is brought to the Temple and has to drink special waters as a test, (Numbers 5:12). The law is that this is not required of converts to Judaism,[6] yet they ruled to the contrary. It may well be that they wanted to impress on all converts that all the *mitzvot* of the Torah applied to them and that they must be as observant as born Jews. It could also be that by their ruling they were trying to elevate the status of converts in the eyes of the rest of the Jews.

Shemayah and Avtalyon were once involved in what can only be described as a very strange incident: Our rabbis taught:

> It once happened that when the High Priest came out of the Temple (on Yom Kippur), all the people started to walk after him (to escort him to his residence). But when the people saw that Shemayah and Avtalyon turned away, they too turned away and followed them instead.[7]

The period in which Shemayah and Avtalyon served on the Sanhedrin was a very difficult one for the Jewish People. Herod, himself the descendent of proselytes, ruled the country with an iron hand, ruthlessly suppressing any sign of opposition to his having usurped the throne. To this end, he also corrupted the exalted office of the *Kohen Gadol*, the High Priesthood. High Priests were appointed and dismissed at the king's will. The office was also for sale[8] and down-right ignoramuses assumed the most important spiritual position in Israel. There were High Priests who were not fit to perform the Yom Kippur service in the Temple and some of them were honest enough to be afraid of entering the Holy of Holies, knowing, as they did, their own deplorable spiritual standard. It is of interest to note that while in the 410 years of the First

Temple only 18 *Kohanim Gedolim* served, in the 420 years of the Second Temple, there were some 300 *Kohanim Gedolim!*[9]

The Mishnah[10] reflects this sorry state of affairs when it tells us that "during the seven days prior to Yom Kippur, the elders of the *Bet Din* (the court), instructed the *Kohen Gadol* in all the procedures of the proper ritual for Yom Kippur.[11] On the eve of Yom Kippur, the court-elders would present him (the High Priest) to the elders of the *kohanim* and as they left they would say, 'We adjure you, O High Priest, not to deviate one iota from what we have taught you.' He turned away and wept and they turned away and wept"[12] The Talmud explains that the High Priest wept because the elders seemed to suspect that he would not perorm the rituals according to the *Halakhah;* the elders wept because they might be suspecting an innocent man."

Another reaction to the condition of the High Priesthood can be discerned in the following *midrash:* On the verse, "And no one shall be in the Sanctuary when he (The High Priest) enters to make atonement (Leviticus 16:17)" Rabbi Simeon commented: "When the Holy Spirit rested on Phinehas his face was as radiant as a fire-brand."[13]

The *piyyut, Mareh Kohen* "The Appearance of the High Priest", which is the central part of our Yom Kippur synagogue service, is based on the poem which Ben Sira composed describing the appearance of Simeon the Tzaddik when he emerged from the Holy of Holies on Yom Kippur day. The face of the *Kohen Gadol* is described as "the clearest canopy of heaven; the wondrous rainbow; the morning star in the east..." All this happened, in the words of the *piyyut,* when "we had a Temple and the High Priest performed his service *as he was obligated to do.* Happy is he who witnessed this."

We can now understand Shemayah and Avtalyon's behavior on that Yom Kippur day. They, together with the rest of the populace, had waited for the dramatic moment when the High Priest would emerge from the Holy of Holies after having made atonement for the Children of Israel. When he came out, Shemayah and Avtalyon immediately realized that the Holy Spirit had not rested on him. He had not performed the ritual properly. His face was not radiant. They would not give him the traditional honor of accompanying him to his house!

The rest of the assembled people were not aware of the tradition in the *midrash* cited above and did not know that something was wrong and so they set out with the *Kohen Gadol*... until they saw their two venerable sages turning away. Then they realized that something had happened and went with them, showing whose authority they trusted. It is highly unlikely that the High Priest let this insult pass without complaining to them. Shemayah and Avtalyon must have retorted: "Love your work. Hate lordship." Perform your duites honestly and faithfully, do not look for honor and grandeur. You did not officiate properly — we will not show you honor.

Seek no intimacy with the ruling power.

The circumstances that brought about this piece of advice can be found in an incident reported by the ancient historian, Josephus, in both his *Antiquities of the Jews* and his *Jewish Wars*,[14] and of which echoes can be found in the Talmud.[15]

Before he usurped the throne, Herod had been governor of the Galilee and, in that capacity, had executed a number of Jews who, he claimed, were bandits. In fact, they were Jewish patriots who objected to the growing Roman influence in the country. The Sanhedrin ordered him to come before it to stand trial and he came dressed in princely robes and accompanied by a contingent of armed soldiers. It was a deliberate affront to the Sanhedrin. He was showing his power and his contempt for the highest court in the land.

Shemayah ordered Herod to send the soldiers away and to divest himself of his royal attire to which he had no right. Herod refused. Shemayah then turned to the other memebers

of the Sanhedrin and asked their opinion. Most of the judges
lowered their heads in embarrassment and remained silent,
either out of fear of Herod or because King Hyrcanus had
asked them not to aggravate an already explosive situation by
judging Herod. Shemayah, in disappointment and anger,
warned them: "You have lowered your heads. One day, Herod
will be king, and he will lower your heads."

And so it happened. When Herod became king he executed
almost all the members of the Sanhedrin because he saw in that
body a permanent reproach to his legitimacy as king.
Shemayah and Avtalyon were among the survivors. Josephus
does not indicate why Herod spared them. It might have been
because of the courage they displayed in standing up to him or
because Shemayah had, in effect, prophesied that Herod would
one day become king. Another reason could be that when
Herod besieged Jerusalem, Shemayah counselled the people to
open the city gates and let him in.

Shemayah and Avtalyon had no fear of Herod and avoided
any contact or intimacy with him. They had their job to do
maintaining the religious life of the people and wanted as little
as possible to do with the wicked king. This may have well been
another piece of advice they offered the High Priest: Do not
become too friendly with the ruling power. Herod appointed
you and may very well replace you as *Kohen Gadol.*

Another interpretation might be: Do not go to Herod and
tell him that we have insulted you. You will have to explain why
and he may well become angry. It is very likely that he will
discharge you and appoint another *Kohen Gadol.*

The encounter with the High Priest did not end with their
turning away. The Talmud continues:

Ultimately Shemayah and Avtalyon went to say goodbye
to the High Priest (i.e., to appease him). He said to them,
"Let the children of the foreign peoples go in peace."
They replied: "May the chilren of the foreign peoples who
do the work of Aaron, the High Priest (i.e., seek peace) go

in peace. But the son of Aaron (i.e., you) who does not do the work of Aaron the High Priest (i.e., rejects their peace overtures) shall not go in peace!"[16]

This was an exceedingly sharp retort particularly taking into consideration that Shemayah and Avtalyon had gone to the High Priest to effect a reconciliation, but it can be understood if we remember the rabbinic attitude to proselytes. Regarding the verse, "And Jethro rejoiced" (Exodus 18:9), Rav remarked: "Do not shame a proselyte, even of the tenth generation, by mentioning his ancestors, the non-Jews!"[17] Shemayah and Avtalyon had come to make their peace with the High Priest although they did not have a high opinion of his qualifications for that exalted office. He had rejected them with an insult that smacked of racism: "Who are you, the descendants of non-Jews, to judge me, a pure-blooded priest." Their answer was truly rabbinic: "Noble is he who noble does. We, the descendants of non-Jews, acted like priests — we wanted to make peace. You, the descendant of priests, did not act as a great grandson of Aaron.

Hillel the Elder, the renowned student of Shemayah and Avtalyon, learned the lesson well. The first of his aphorisms is: "Be of the disciples of Aaron, loving peace and pursuing peace, loving your fellow creatures and bringing them near to Torah."[18] It is interesting to note that Hillel did not say "your fellow Jews," but rather "your fellow creatures" which means even Gentiles. He knew only too well what non-Jews were capable of producing — men like Shemayah and Avtalyon.

Avtalyon said: Sages, be careful with your words lest you incur the penalty of exile and be exiled to a place of evil waters, and the students who follow you will drink of them and die and the Heavenly Name will be profaned.[19]

Avtalyon's advice to his colleagues was also occasioned by the circumstances of the times. Herod's massacre of the Sanhedrin must have made many sages flee to other countries, places of "evil water," i.e., foreign philosophies and alien cultures. The sages themselves would be able to withstand negative influences and remain good Jews; but the students, who would follow them to learn Torah, would be exposed to inducements and temptations too strong for them to reject. Avtalyon, although anxious about the fate of the sages, was more concerned for their disciples. The Bertinoro's interpretation of Avtalyon's name, cited at the beginning of this chapter, is therefore very fitting: The father of children, i.e., students.

We have seen how the dicta of these two outstanding sages, Shemayah and Avtalyon, become so much more significant when viewed against the background of their historical period and their own lives.

Notes

1. *Avot* 1:10
2. *Gittin* 57b
3. *Sanhedrin* 36b
4. *TJ Horayot* 1:4
5. *Avot* 1:10, Bertinoro's commentary
6. *Eduyyot* 5:6
7. *Yoma* 71b
8. *Midrash Rabbah, Leviticus* 21:9
9. *Yoma* 9a. The *midrash*, however, has it that ther were some 80 High Priests in the Second Temple
10. *Mishnah Yoma* 2a
11. *Mishnah Yoma* 18a
12. *Mishnah Yoma* 18b-19b
13. *Midrash Rabbah, Leviticus* 21:12
14. Josephus, *Antiquities* 14:9:4, *Wars* 1:10:7
15. *Bava Batra* 4a
16. *Yoma* 71b
17. *Sanhedrin* 94a
18. *Avot* 1:12
19. *Avot* 1:11

Hillel

הִלֵּל וְשַׁמַּאי קִבְּלוּ מֵהֶם. הִלֵּל אוֹמֵר: הֱוֵי מִתַּלְמִידָיו שֶׁל אַהֲרֹן,
אוֹהֵב שָׁלוֹם, וְרוֹדֵף שָׁלוֹם, אוֹהֵב אֶת הַבְּרִיּוֹת, וּמְקָרְבָן לַתּוֹרָה.

*Hillel and Shammai received the tradition from them
(Shemayah and Avtalyon). Hillel says: "Be of the disciples
of Aaron, the first Kohen Gadol, loving peace, pursuing
peace, loving your fellow men, and drawing them near to
Torah."*[1]

Hillel is credited in the first and second chapters of Avot with
several deep and important dicta and it is interesting to note
that Rabbi Judah the Nasi, the redactor of the Mishnah, chose
this particular one to introduce Hillel to the reader. The reason
is that this dictum personifies Hillel's character - love for all
humanity. The Talmud presents Hillel as an example to all men
and sets him off against his illustrious but somewhat short-
tempered colleague, Shammai. "Always be as gentle as Hillel,"
teaches the Talmud, "and not as impatient as Shammai!"[2] The
Talmud continues to recount a number of incidents in which
Hillel and Shammai were involved which tend to verify this
pithy characterization.

Two incidents are very typical.[3] On one occasion a certain
man made a wager of 400 zuz (an exceedingly large sum) that
he could cause Hillel to lose his temper. Such was Hillel's
reputation that men bet on his forbearance. It was a Friday
afternoon and Hillel was washing his hair in preparation for
the Sabbath when the gambler passed by his door and called
out, "Is there a Hillel here? Is there a Hillel here?" This

behavior was the height of impudence; Hillel was the president of the Sanhedrin and, in effect, one of the two most important men in the land and this man called him by his given name without any title. Hillel dressed himself and went out to his visitor.

"My son, what do you want?"

"I have a question to ask."

"Ask, my son."

"Why are the heads of the Babylonians elongated?"

Besides being a foolish question, this was a deliberate insult, for Hillel himself was a Babylonian.

"My son, you have asked an important question. The reason is that their midwives are not expert."

The fellow went away, waited a while and returned. Again he called out, "Is there a Hillel here? Is there a Hillel here?" and once again Hillel dressed and came out to him.

"My son, what do you want?"

"I have a question to ask."

"Ask, my son."

"Why are the eyes of the Palmyreans weak?"

"My son, you have asked an important question. The reason is that they live in sandy places."

Once more, the man waited a while and then returned, following the same insolent procedure.

"Why are the feet of Africans wide?"

"My son, you have asked an important question. It is because they live in marshy country and they need wide feet to be able to walk."

At this, the gambler said:

"I have many questions to ask but I am afraid that you will become angry."

Hillel dressed himself and sat down with his visitor.

"Ask all the questions you want."

"Are you the Hillel who is called the Nasi of Israel?"

"Yes."

"If that is you, may there not be many like you in Israel!"

"Why, my son?"

"Because I have lost 400 zuz because of you!"

"Control yourself. Hillel is worth it that you should lose 400 zuz and yet another 400 zuz and that Hillel should not lose his temper!"

The Talmud also tells of three heathens who came to Shammai to be converted to Judaism - but "on condition." Shammai drove them away but Hillel found ways to reconcile them and they became good Jews. Perhaps the most famous of these cases was the following: On another occasion it happened that a heathen came before Shammai and said to him, "Convert me to Judaism on condition that you teach me the whole Torah while I stand on one foot. Shammai drove him away with the mason's measuring rod that he was holding. When the heathen came before Hillel, he converted him by stating "What is hateful to you, do not do to your fellow! That is the whole Torah; the rest is commentary - go and study !"[4]

Hillel's answer to the proselyte has puzzled students ever since. Why did he coin his own principle in the negative, "What is hateful to you, do not do..." when there is a perfectly good positive form of the same idea in the Torah itself "Love your neighbor as yourself" (Leviticus 19:18)?

There can be no doubt that this convert presented Hillel with a serious problem. On the one hand Hillel saw before him a person who wanted to be a Jew, but on the other hand what could he teach him while standing on one foot? The laws of the Shabbat? The laws of Pesah? The laws of ritual purity? Clearly not. Hillel decided to teach him the cardinal law of behavior between human beings, the laws of *bein adam le-havero*. He insisted, however, that this is Torah, divine law, and not mere social convention. Thus the convert, by accepting this formulation was in fact accepting God's sovereignty and the supremacy of His Torah.

Hillel's choice of the negative formulation was quite

deliberate. When a gentile is converted, he leaves his previous society of other non-Jews completely but he has not yet become integrated into Jewish society nor does he yet have Jewish friends. Hillel could not tell him, "Love your neighbor" because the convert did not have "neighbors" in the Jewish society; but Hillel could - and did - teach him, "What is hateful to you do not do..." because that is independent of others, has universal implications and applies directly to him.[4]

The Talmud closes the three incidents of the proselytes with a remarkable anecdote. The three converts once met and in discussing their conversion to Judaism came to the conclusion that "Shammai's impatience would have driven us from the world, but Hillel's patience brought us under the wings of the *Shekhinah*."[5]

Hillel was also blessed with an extraordinary understanding of human beings and sympathetic to their needs even at the cost of his own comfort and dignity. The Talmud interprets the verse,[6] "When there be among you a poor man... you must not harden your heart or close your hand... but you must give him sufficient for his need which he needs"(Deuteronomy 15:8-9), in the following manner: "sufficient for his need" - you are commanded to support him but you are not required to make him rich; "which he needs" - even a horse to ride and a servant to run before him! The Talmud then continues: "They used to say about Hillel the Elder that he once bought a horse and a slave for a poor man who came from a wealthy family (and who had become impoverished). Once, when he could not find a slave, he, Hillel, ran before him for a distance of three miles."

In his great insight into human nature, Hillel realized that for this poor man a horse and a slave were as important as food and clothing for other people. This pauper had once been wealthy and his ego needed these signs of affluence, these status symbols. Charity, as Hillel understood it, means giving the supplicant what *he* needs, not what *you* think he should need and Hillel, the Nasi of all Israel, was prepared to give him that even if he had to run before him himself!

Hillel's concern for the unfortunate was not, however, confined to his personal activities. As a legislator, he was responsible for one of the most revolutionary *takkanot*, special laws, in Jewish history. The Torah (Deuteronomy 15:1) rules that in the seventh year, *shemittah*, all debts are cancelled and this of course led to a state of affairs in which people would not lend money during the period before the *shemittah* year out of fear that they would lose it. For people in need of credit this created very great hardship and Hillel instituted a regulation, known as *prozbul*, in force to this very day, by which the lender made out a statement of intent addressed to the court before the end of the seventh year, and which enabled the debt to be collected afterwards.[7]

Hillel's second "social" *takkanah* was with regard to the sale of houses in walled cities. According to the Torah, "If a man sells a dwelling in a walled city, he can redeem it (i.e., buy it back) until the end of the year from the time of the sale" (Leviticus 25:29). What used to happen was that the buyer, who wanted to keep the property permanently, would disappear on the last day of the year so that the seller would not be able to find him and pay back the purchase price. Hillel ruled that the seller could deposit the money in the Temple treasury and that this constituted payment to the buyer.[8]

No wonder then that Rabbi Judah cited as the first of Hillel's teachings: "Love peace. Love your fellow men!"

He (Hillel) used to say: "If I am not for myself, who will be for me? But if I am only for myself, what am I? And if not now, when?[9] According to the sources, Hillel was a descendant of King David.[10] He was born in Babylonia. Indeed, in the Talmud he is also called "Hillel the Babylonian."[11] The Jewish community in Babylonia was established following the destruction of the First Temple in 586 B.C.E., and the large number of Jews who were exiled there organized their lives as a separate, autonomous community. They established all the institutions necessary for Jewish life including *yeshivot*.[12] The prophet Ezra, who led the return to Eretz Israel, is said to have been a student of Barukh ben Neriah who was the Prophet Jeremiah's secretary. Not all the Jews in Babylonia returned with Ezra and, from that time on, the two large centers of Jewish life, Eretz Israel and Babylonia, existed side by side.

It is not known who the teachers of Hillel in Babylonia were, but we do know that he heard of Shemayah and Avtalyon in Jerusalem and made up his mind to go there to further his *Torah* studies. "If I am not for myself, who will be for me?" He left his home in Babylonia and went up to Jerusalem.

Shemayah and Avtalyon required students in their *yeshivah* to pay a daily tuition fee.[13] There were two reasons for this. Firstly, it helped maintain the institution and secondly it discouraged dilettantes who were not serious students. Hillel found work as a day laborer and used half his earnings to support his family and the rest was spent on his tuition fees. One Friday during the winter, he had no money, and the gate keeper of the *yeshivah* refused to admit him. Hillel climbed onto the roof and stationed himself at the skylight "in order to hear the words of the living God from the mouth of Shemayah and Avtalyon." It began to snow but Hillel was so engrossed that he did not move and almost froze. On the following morning, Shabbat, Shemayah and Avtalyon noticed that it was darker than usual in the study hall. When they raised their glance towards the skylight they noticed a figure spread out on the skylight, and so Hillel was found, covered by three cubits of snow. They dug him out, washed and massaged him and sat him near the fire although it was Shabbat. "For such a one as this," they said, "it is permitted to desecrate the Sabbath!"[13]

How long Hillel studied at the *yeshivah* of Shemayah and Avtalyon is unknown. However, when he had absorbed all he could, he returned to his native Babylonia to teach there what he had learned in Jerusalem. " "If I am only for myself, what am I?"

Hillel had a brother, Shevna, who was a merchant.[14] Shevna offered him a business proposition: he, Shevna, would share the profits of his business with Hillel and Hillel would agree that he, Shevna, would receive half the reward for Hillel's Torah study! This was based on the midrashic explanation of Moses' blessing: "Rejoice, Zevulun, in your going out (business) and Issachar in your tents (Torah study)" (Deuteronomy,33:18). As poor as he was, Hillel refused the offer. Studying Torah was too important for him to cede even a portion of its reward. Hillel's attitude to learning Torah is aptly summed up in another *mishnah* in Avot: "Do not say 'I will study when I have time.' Perhaps you will never have time!"[15] The Talmud tells us that when Shevna made his proposition, a voice called from heaven and quoted the verse, "If a man would offer all the treasure of his house..." The offer would be despised (Songs of Songs 8:7).[14]

Hillel remained in Babylonia for some time teaching Torah but after a while he felt the need to return to Jerusalem. There was nobody in Babylonia to whom he could turn for guidance in his own studies and he was perplexed by a number of questions. So he decided to return to Eretz Israel. "If not now, when?"

With the death of Shemayah and Avtalyon, the level of scholarship in Eretz Israel had deteriorated considerably. King Herod had killed most of the Sanhedrin[16] and had appointed some unknown scholars, called the Benei Bathyra, Sons of Bathyra, as the religious leadership. These were men of limited knowledge and they are not mentioned in Avot as the stage between Shemayah and Avtalyon and Hillel and Shammai. Even their individual names are nowhere recorded although there are later *tannaim*, such as Rabbi Judah ben Bathyra, who seem to have been descendants of this family. Except for the incident with Hillel, the Benei Bathyra left no mark in either **Halachah** or **Aggadah**. There is, however, one incident which might be seen as referring to them. On the question of what happened to the people resurrected in the "Dry Bones" prophecy of Ezekiel (37:1-14), Rabbi Eliezer the son of Rabbi Yose Ha-Galilee said: "The dead whom Ezekiel resurrected went up to Eretz Israel, married women and sired sons and daughters." At this, Rabbi Judah ben Bathyra stood up and said: "I am one of their descendants and these are the *tefillin* that my grandfather left me as a heirloom from them."[17]

Josephus records[18] that Herod had built a city in northern Trans-Jordan called Bathyra and many Babylonian Jews settled there because of the tax advantages they were offered. The residents of the city acted as guards for the caravans of pilgrims coming from Babylonia to Jerusalem to offer their sacrifices in the Temple. They were able warriors and served as one of Herod's insurance policies against internal revolt and foreign invasion. It is assumed that the Benei Bathyra who stood at the head of the Sanhedrin were members of this city's distinguished families.

It happened that the first day of Passover fell on Sunday, and on the previous Friday the Benei Bathyra were in a quandary. Normally the Paschal Lamb is slaughtered on the day before Passover, the 14th day of Nissan. Was the slaughter of the Lamb permitted on the Sabbath? A certain person told them. "There is a man here from Babylonia, Hillel the Babylonian is his name, who studied with the two greatest sages of the age, Shemayah and Avtalyon and he knows whether the Paschal Lamb may be slaughtered on Shabbat." They called Hillel and asked him. He ruled that it could be slaughtered on Shabbat and even proved it by brilliant pieces of scriptural exegesis.[19]

The Benei Bathyra were honest men and realized that here was a scholar immeasurably greater than they, and so they relinquished their positions as head of the Sanhedrin and appointed Hillel as *Nasi*. Hillel spent the rest of the day instructing the people in the laws of Passover and castigated the Benei Bathyra for their ignorance, claiming that they had not attended Shemayah and Avtalyon (sufficiently) and thus were not well-learned. Hillel's descendant, the famous Rabbi Judah the Nasi, praised what the Benei Bathyra did in favor of his grandfather, Hillel, they resigned their position in his favour.[20] The Talmud records that Hillel was appointed *Nasi* one hundred years before the destruction of the Temple, i.e., in 30 B.C.E., and that he held the position for forty years.[21]

Hillel was never ashamed to admit, "I have forgotten this law," and when he later recalled the particular halakhah he would say humbly, "Thus did I hear from my teachers."[22] He was also careful to transmit his teachers' traditions in their own words: "A person should always speak in the language of his teachers."[23]

In his method of learning and expounding the Torah, Hillel was an innovator. He was one of the first to apply the seven hermeneutical principles of explaining the words of the Torah (*Ha-midot she-ha-Torah nidreshet bahen*) to the practical Halakhah. In the account of his conversation with the Benei вathyra in the Babylonian Talmud,[24] Hillel used three of the hermeneutical principles to make his point. Another source[25] has it that hillel explained the seven hermeneutical principles to the Benei Bathyra.

In addition to his enormous erudition and humility, Hillel was also blessed with a sense of humor which he used to get his teachings across forcefully. We are told[26] that when Hillel left his students he used to go off for a walk. They asked him where he was going and he replied, "To perform a *mitzvah*." Wanting to learn from all their teacher's ways, they asked him which *mitzvah*." Hillel told them that he was going to take a bath and they asked further, "Is that a *mitzvah*?" To which Hillel replied, "Well if the statues of kings in the theaters and circuses are washed and cleaned by those in charge of them, how much more so must we, who are created in God's image, take care of our bodies."

Hillel's elevation to the presidency of the Sanhedrin brought about a tremendous upswing in Torah learning and his influence was felt for centuries. Of the disciples he raised, the Talmud[27] says: "Hillel had 80 students; 30 of them were great enough for the *Shekhinah* to rest upon them as it did on Moses; 30 were great enough for the sun to stand still for them as it did for Joshua; 20 were average scholars. The greatest of the students was Jonathan ben Uziel and the youngest student was Johanan ben Zakai."

The sages of the Talmud expressed their evaluation of Hillel's contribution to Jewish life thus: "In the beginning, when the Torah was forgotten in Israel, Ezra came up from Babylonia and established it. Later, when it was forgotten again, Hillel the Babylonian came up and restored it..."[28]

He (Hillel) used to say: "A boor cannot be a sin-fearing person nor can an ignoramus be truly pious. A shy person cannot learn nor can a quick-tempered one teach."[29]

This statement illustrates that, notwithstanding his patience and piety, Hillel was an exceedingly level-headed thinker. He realized the importance of intellect and learning and was, in fact, saying, that heart alone is not enough. Considering the role Hillel played in the re-establishment of a high standard of Torah learning in Eretz Israel, this dictum can almost be seen as a statement of policy.

Although the last part of the aphorism could be understood as a reference to Shammai, whose short temper has already been indicated above, it must be remembered that Shammai also founded a major academy of Torah learning, Bet Shammai, which is always mentioned in the sources together with Hillel's *yeshivah*, Bet Hillel. It must also be borne in mind that Shammai himself is quoted in Avot as saying: "Receive all men cheerfully!"[30]

Shammai, as we shall see in Chapter 9, was short-tempered only when he believed that the dignity and sanctity of the Torah were at question. Thus, his attitude to the three applicants for conversion. If you come to Torah, you must accept it totally and unconditionally. Human nature and ego must be subservient to Torah! This also applies to his attitude to his students. In his personal life, however, he was a very kind-hearted person.

Moreover, he (Hillel) saw a skull floating on the surface of the water. He said to it: "Because you drowned others, they drowned you; and ultimately those who drowned you will be drowned."[31]

According to Josephus,[32] this monologue, which is also quoted in the Gemara,[33] was directed at the skull of Aristobulus, the grandson of Hyrcanus, the last of the Hasmonean family. King Herod had invited Aristobulus to his palace near Jericho and while he was bathing in the palace pool, Herod had him drowned.

Herod was a vicious paranoic. He suspected everybody of plotting against him and killed indiscriminately, even members of his own immediate family.[34] His wife, Mariamne of the royal Hasmonean dynasty, his mother-in-law, his sons and many of his closest friends all fell victim to his sick suspicions that they were conspiring to depose him. His mad behavior was even the subject of a *bon mot* of the Roman emperor, Augustus. "I would rather be Herod's pig," he said, "than his son!" The point was that Herod did not eat pork and so his pig stood a chance of staying alive!

The thought that seeing the skull aroused in Hillel a warning to Herod and the whole murderous system of government. 'He who lives by the sword will die by it!' This idea is also an extension of what Hillel taught the convert: "What is hateful to you, do not do to your fellow." Because, if you do to your fellow that which is hateful to you, ultimately somebody else will do it to you!

Like their predecessors at the head of the Sanhedrin, Hillel and Shammai also differed over whether the "laying on of hands" ceremony in the Temple should be performed on a festival.[35] This question had split the first *zug*, Yose ben Yoezer and Yose ben Johanan, and had continued to be a point of difference between the members of every one of the *zugot*. Shammai claimed that since burnt-offerings were not eaten by human beings but entirely consumed on the altar, the act of laying on of hands, which was considered work, was not "needed for human consumption" and was therefore forbidden on a festival. Hillel argued that "God's consumption" could certainly not be considered less important than human consumption and that it should therefore be permitted.

The Talmud[36] records the following incident:

It once happened that Hillel the Elder brought an *olah* (a burnt offering) to the Temple courtyard on a festival to perform the "laying on of hands" ceremony. A group of Shammai the Elder's disciples gathered round him. "What sort of animal is this?" they demanded to know. Hillel, anxious to avoid conflict said, "It is a female animal, (only male animals are acceptable for burnt-offerings) and I have brought it for a peace-offering" (which is eaten by the person who offers it). This was a white lie made, according to Rashi, in order to preserve the peace. The animal wagged its tail as though to verify Hillel's statement. Shammai's students were satisfied and went away. On that day the influence of Bet Shammai increased over that of Bet Hillel (in the Sanhedrin) and Bet Shammai insisted that the law be fixed in accordance with their opinion.

At the session, an old sage Bava ben Buta was present. He had been a student of Shammai the Elder but he knew that the law is according to Bet Hillel. He sent and brought to the Temple courtyard all the flocks of Kedar sheep (a very good breed) that were in Jerusalem. "Let everyone who wants to perform the "laying on of hands" ceremony come and perform it and, of course, offer the sheep as an *olah*". On that day, Bet Hillel's influence prevailed and the law was fixed according to them and there was no one who objected.

Although the law is generally decided in accordance with the opinions of Bet Hillel, there are exceptions when Bet

Shammai's rulings are accepted. In the academy it seems that
Bet Shammai was the majority, but the Talmud[37] records that
Bet Hillel and Bet Shammai argued for three years about
whose opinion should be law. Finally, a voice from heaven
declared: "These and these are the words of the living God! But
the law is in accordance with Bet Hillel!" The Talmud asks,
"Since both are the words of the living God, why did Bet Hillel
merit that the law is in accordance with it's opinion?" The
answer is, "Because they, Bet Hillel, were mild and tolerant
and taught Bet Shammai's views as well as their own."

However, the Talmud[38] cites one case in which not only was
Shammai's view accepted but Hillel was caused considerable
embarrassment:
When one harvests grapes for the vat (i.e., to make wine),
Shammai said: They (the grapes) become fit to become unclean
(by virtue of their becoming wet) but Hillel ruled that they do
not become fit to become unclean. Said Hillel to Shammai,
"Why must one gather grapes in purity (so that they do not
become impure, according to Shammai's view) yet not need to
gather olives in purity (even according to Shammai)?" "If you
provoke me," Shammai replied to him, "I will decree
uncleanness in the case of olive gathering too."

A sword was planted in the study hall and it was proclaimed:
"He who would enter, let him enter; but he who would depart,
let him not depart." This was the practice whenever a vote was
to be taken. On that day Hillel sat submissive before Shammai
like one of the students and it (that day) was as grievous to
Israel as the day the golden calf was made (because Hillel, the
Nasi, was insulted).

The differences of opinion between the two great schools
were not confined to Halakhic matters but embraced theology
and philosophy. We are told[39] that they discussed one
philosophical principle for two and one half years before
taking a vote which also went against Bet Hillel's view. The
question was whether it would have been better for man not to

have been created. Bet Hillel took the optimistic view that it was better for man to have been created but Bet Shammai argued that it would have been better for him if he had not been created. Finally they took a vote and the decision was: It would have been better for man not to have been created, but now that he has been created let him examine his ways.

Unfortunately, no record of the actual discussions on this question has reached us but it is possible that the final conclusion was reached because in the Torah there are more negative commandments ("You shall not...") than positive ones ("You shall..."). Of the former there are three hundred and sixty five while of the latter sort there are two hundred and forty eight. The Almighty Himself said after the Flood, "I will never again curse the earth because of man, for the inclination of the heart of man is evil from his youth" (Genesis 8:21). Thus the tendency to do evil is stronger than the desire to do good. Therefore, it would have been better for man if he had not been created at all.

The Talmud[40] also tells us of a difference in customs between Hillel and Shammai which, although it does not seem very important grew out of a basic difference in their outlooks. They (the sages) said about Shammai the Elder, "All his days he used to eat in honor of the Sabbath! If he came across a fine animal (or any other choice food) he would say, 'This is for Shabbat!' If he then found a better one, he would put it aside for Shabbat and eat the former one. But Hillel had a different approach. All his deeds were for the sake of Heaven, as it is written, 'Blessed be God, who every day loads us with benefits...' (Psalms 68:20).

Shammai would start preparing for Shabbat from the preceding Sunday and for him the whole week existed only for the sake of Shabbat. Hillel, in his deep faith, took life day by day, sure that the Almighty would provide for the Sabbath as He does for all man's daily needs.

May we know the faith of Hillel, - to love and seek peace, to study Torah and to rely upon the Almighty for our daily requirements.

Notes

1. *Avot* 1:12
2. *Shabbat* 30b
3. *Ibid* 31a
4. *Ibid*
5. I am indebted to Ha-Rav Ha-Gaon Rabbi Abraham Kroll for this explanation.
6. *Ketubbot* 67b
7. *Gittin* 34b, 36a
8. *Arakhin* 31b (31b)
9. *Avot* 1:14
10. *TJ Kilayim* 9:3; *TJ Taanit* 4:2 *Midrash Rabbah, Genesis* . 98:13.
11. *Pesahim* 66a
12. *Megillah* 16b
13. *Yoma* 35b
14. *Sotah* 21a
15. *Avot* 2:5
16. Josephus, *Antiquities*, 14:9.4
17. *Sanhedrin* 92b
18. Josephus, *Ibid.*, 17:2:2
19. *Pesahim* 66a
20. *TJ Kilayim* 9:3; *P'nay Moshe, T.J. Ketuboth* 12:3
21. *Sifre Dvorim Broho* 356
22. *Pesahim* 66a
23. *Eduyot* 1:3
24. *Pesahim* 66a
25. *Tosefta, Sanhedrin* 7:5
26. *Midrash Rabbah, Lev. 34:3*
27. *Sukkah* 28a
28. *Ibid*, 20a

29. *Avot* 2:6
30. *Ibid*, 1:15
31. *Ibid*, 2:7
32. Josephus, *Antiquities*, 15:3:3
33. *Sukkah* 53a
34. Josephus, *Antiquities*, 15:7.4
35. *Bezah* 20a/b; *TJ Hagigah* 2:3
36. *Bezah* 20a/b
37. *Eruvin* 13b
38. *Shabbat* 7a
39. *Eruvin* 13b
40. *Bezah* 16a

Menachem

It is generally accepted that there were five zugot, pairs of Sages of whom Yose ben Yoezer and Yose Ben Johanan were the first (Chap.3,4) and Hillel and Shammai were the last. (chap.7-9). Of each of these pairs, one served as the Nasi, President, of the Sanhedrin and the other as Av Bet Din, the head of the court. In Avot no mention is made of a Tanna Menahem, who was Av Bet Din when Hillel was appointed Nasi.

In the *mishnah*,[1] however, Menahem is mentioned and we are told that he did not disagree with Hillel on the question of "laying on of hands" on a festival, over which question all the previous *zugot* had disagreed. "Hillel and Menahem did not disagree. Menahem went out and Shammai came in.[2] Shammai ruled not to perform the ceremony, Hillel ruled to perform it."

The Gemara[2] takes note of the phrasing of the *mishnah*, "Menahem went out," and asks, "Where did he go?" To this there are two answers. Abbaye said that "he went out to evil ways," and Rava said that "he went out to the king's service and with him went 80 pairs of students dressed in silken robes." Rashi explains the "silken robes" as royal apparel.

The same matter is discussed in the Jerusalem Talmud[3] but with significant changes and additions:

Where did he go? Some say he went from one way of life to another; others say that he went out against his will, together with 80 pairs of scholars dressed in golden robes, because they (the non-Jews) blackened their (the Jews') faces as black as the side of a cooking pot, saying to them, "Write it on the horn of an ox that you have no part in the God of Israel!"

The *Korban Ha-Edah*, one of the classical commentaries on the Jerusalem Talmud, explains that Menahem and the 80 pairs of scholars left the Sanhedrin in order to combat anti-semitism which manifested itself in the non-Jews claiming that God had deserted Israel and that every Jew who had an ox should inscribe that on its horn as a method of publicizing the matter. It is also possible, however, that the non-Jews were mocking the Jews by telling them to write the message on the horns of animals that were offered in the Temple, as much as to say: "You are bringing sacrifices to God who pays no attention to you. He has rejected you." For this reason the scholars dressed in royal attire to show the gentiles that they still believed in God and were sure that all would be well for Israel because they were God's children -- Princes.

These passages in the Talmud would seem to indicate that, according to Rava, Menahem left his judicial and scholarly position as *Av Bet Din* reluctantly in order to engage in communal work of a different nature, apparently in external relations with the non-Jewish, Hellenistic population of Eretz Israel. For this purpose he took with him the 160 students as his assistants.

Josephus,[4] however, tells a different story. Menahem was an Essene, a member of that extremely strict and ascetic sect that arose during the Second Temple era. Menahem had met Herod when the latter was a child and had prophesied that he would one day be king. Menahem had even given the boy, Herod, a paternal pat on his backside and told him, "Remember, when you are king, be pious and love and do justice." Menahem, however, had known in his heart that this would not be, and that Herod would be a cruel and evil king.

When Herod became king, he remembered the prophecy and called Menahem from his position in the Sanhedrin to join the royal household. Nothing further is known of Menahem but we do know that Herod favored the Essenes. This might have been because of Menahem's influence or because Herod realized that the Essenes, with their monastic, withdrawn life-style, did not constitute a threat to him.

Herod was a cruel and bloodthirsty tyrant who showed no mercy to his family and friends, let alone his enemies. It is therefore legitimate to imagine that Menahem accepted Herod's invitation to join the royal household out of fear for his life. This might be the circumstance which called forth Hillel's dictum,[5] "Do not separate yourself from the community." Hillel was addressing himself directly to Menahem, begging him not to join Herod's entourage where he would have to be a party to executing the king's evil intentions.

Even if we accept the opinion that Menahem "went out" to join the Essenes, Hillel's aphorism fits him perfectly. The Essenes were separatists who were concerned only with their own spiritual welfare. Hillel might very well have been pleading with his colleague, "Do not secede from the general community which needs your guidance and leadership."

Wherever Menachem went, his leaving the second most important post in the Sanhedrin must have aroused a great deal of comment among the Jews. Many of the self-righteous no doubt criticised him severely claiming that they would never have done such a thing; that they would rather suffer death than give up their religious affiliation or that they would never leave the general community. Hillel could very well have been talking to these critics when he continued, "Do not believe in yourself until the day you die and do not judge your fellow man until you are in his position!"[5] Who knows why Menahem did what he did? Which person can be sure how he would behave if the same pressures and temptations - both physical and psychological - as were applied to Menahem were applied to him? The glitter of royal power and influence or despair at the contemporary situation may have led Menahem to "go out."

Some scholars[6] have identified Menahem with Menahem ben Judah the Galilean who was one of the Zealot leaders in the revolt against Rome which led to the destruction of the

Second Temple. This Menahem, dressed in royal attire, was assassinated in the Temple by a rival Zealot faction and his relative, Eleazar ben Yair, fled with Menahem's followers to Masada, where ultimately they killed themselves rather than fall into Roman hands.

This identification is, however, very problematic since Menahem was *Av Bet Din* when Hillel was appointed *Nasi*, one hundred years before the destruction of the Temple!

Menahem did not leave any statements in *Halakhah* or *Aggadah* and all that we know of him is that he agreed with Hillel on the "laying on of hands" question and that "Menahem went out and Shammai came in."

Notes

1. *Hagigah* 16a
2. *Hagigah* 16b
3. *TJ Hagigah* 2:2
4. Josephus, *Antiquities* 15:10:4
5. *Avot* 2:5
6. Ha-Enziklopedia Ha-Ivrit, vol.22, 1024　Encyclopaedia Judaica, vol.11, p.1308,1313.s.v. Menahem the Essene; Menahem son of Judah

Shammai

שַׁמַּאי אוֹמֵר: עֲשֵׂה תוֹרָתְךָ קֶבַע, אֱמֹר מְעַט וַעֲשֵׂה הַרְבֵּה, וֶהֱוֵי מְקַבֵּל אֶת כָּל הָאָדָם בְּסֵבֶר פָּנִים יָפוֹת.

Shammai said: "Make your Torah study a regular habit; say little and do much; and receive all men with a cheerful countenance."[1]

Very little is known of Hillel's great colleague, Shammai. We do not know where or when he was born. It seems that he, like Hillel, studied under Shemayah and Avtalyon, because the *mishnah* records that he, together with Hillel, received the tradition from them.[2] Nor do we know how old Shammai was when he became *Av Bet Din* or when he died. In Talmudic sources[3] he is called Shammai the Elder which might indicate that he lived to a ripe old age. It seems that by profession he was a builder since he is described as holding a builder's measuring rod.[4]

Unlike Hillel who left a son, Simeon,[5] to succeed him as *Nasi* of the Sanhedrin, Shammai left no official successor and, as far as we know, his lineage stopped with him, whereas Hillel founded a scholastic dynasty which flourished for centuries.

We have already made reference to Shammai's reverence for the Sabbath in Chapter 7 and it is interesting to note that he even forbade sending a letter with a non-Jew unless there was enough time for the letter to arrive at its destination before Shabbat so that the Shabbat should not be desecrated even by the hand of the non-Jew.[6] However, on the question of the conduct of a war to occupy Eretz Israel, Shammai ruled that if the siege of a city started before Shabbat, it should be continued until it succeeds, even on the Sabbath. The reason for this is that the conquest and settlement of Eretz Israel is a *mitzvah* as it is written: "And you may build siegeworks against the city that is at war with you until it falls" (Deuteronomy 20:20), which Shammai interprets as meaning "even on the Sabbath."[7] Sending a letter, however, is a different matter; there is no element of *mitzvah* involved and certainly not a *mitzvah* with the national implications of the settlement of Eretz Israel, and therefore the sanctity of the Sabbath must take precedence.

Shammai's love of Torah study and the performance of its commandments filled his very being. Realizing that not everybody can afford the luxury of totally devoting himself to Torah study, he therefore instructs us to set aside a fixed period daily for that purpose. This applies to all Jews according to their circumstances and ability; to the poor as well as to the rich, to the laborer as well as to the employer.

One of the problems of Torah study is the different opinions that one finds in the Mishnah and the Gemara. According to the Talmud,[8] these disagreements began in the times of Hillel and Shammai and are due to "the students who did not apply themselves dilligently enough to their studies." Furthermore, we often find sages who are strict in their interpretation with regard to some laws and lenient with regard to others. Indeed, Hillel and Shammai themselves are very good examples of this phenomenon. Throughout the Talmud we learn that Hillel is more lenient in his rulings than Shammai, but we also find instances where Shammai is the more lenient.

A special section in the Mishnah[9] lists the laws on which Bet Shammai took the more lenient view. The Gemara[10] comments:

> The law is according to Bet Hillel but he who wants to act in accordance with Bet Shammai may do so and he who wants to go according to Bet Hillel may do so. If a person follows the lenient rulings of Bet Shammai and the lenient

rulings of Bet Hillel, he is wicked; if he goes according to the strict rulings of Bet Shammai and the strict rulings of Bet Hillel, he is the person referred to in the verse: "The fool walks in darkness." (Ecclesiastes 2:14).

Rabban Gamaliel, the grandson of Hillel, had this state of affairs in mind when he taught: "Provide yourself with a teacher (*rav*) and avoid doubt."[11] Each person must choose his *rav* and then follow his decisions consistently whether *le-kulah* (lenient) or *le-humrah* (strict), and not go from one authority to the other looking for more lenient or stricter decisions.

Shammai's dictum in our *mishnah* can also be understood as a directive to rabbis and teachers. "Make your Torah fixed" -- do not teach one thing and practice another. Shammai was a strict teacher but he himself lived by the high standards he demanded of others. The Mishnah[12] rules that women, slaves and minors are exempt from the obligation of living in the *sukkah*, yet when Shammai's daughter-in-law gave birth to a boy during the festival of Sukkot, Shammai broke away the plaster of the roof over his grandson's crib and covered the hole he made with *sekhah* (*sukkah* covering) for the sake of the infant, because he, Shammai, rules that all males, even newborn infants, are obliged to eat and live in the *sukkah*, during the Sukkot festival.

Another instance of this insistence on consistency occurred on Yom Kippur.[13] The law is that one must not wash oneself on that holy day. Another law is that one must not feed another person without first washing one's hands to avoid transferring ritual impurity. Shammai, therefore, refused to feed his son, who was a minor and not obligated to fast on Yom Kippur. It was only when the other sages rebuked him that he finally agreed to wash his hands and feed the child.

Shammai's teaching, "Say little and do much," was a faithful expression of his own character and such a way of life attracted many devoted students notwithstanding his strictness. Most commentators[14] on the *mishnah* cite the incident of Abraham and the angels (Genesis 18:1-8) as the classic example of "saying little and doing much." Abraham invited the three wayfarers into his tent "for a little water and a morsel of bread" and then prepared for them a banquet fit for kings.

And receive all men with a cheerful countenance.[1]

This teaching of Shammai is extraordinary when it is considered in the light of the advice the Talmud[15] gives: "Always be as gentle as Hillel and not as impatient as Shammai." Would we expect an "impatient" teacher to exhort his students to receive *all* men with a cheerful countenance, even nuisances and ignoramuses?

Furthermore, Shammai established an outstanding *yeshivah* which was one of the main sources of Torah study for generations, and which apparently attracted more students than did the *yeshivah* of Hillel. Yet Hillel proclaimed that "a quick-tempered person cannot teach."[16] With regard to Shammai's *yeshivah* the Talmud[17] records that a voice came from heaven and announced that the teachings of Bet Shammai and Bet Hillel were both "the words of the living God." Nevertheless, Bet Shammai was founded and inspired by this quick-tempered Shammai.

The solution to this enigma is that Shammai was impatient and quick-tempered only when the dignity of the Torah was involved (see Chapter 7); he would brook no compromise with regard to the word of God. In his view, the human ego had to be entirely subservient to the demands of the Torah and no concessions could be made. However, in his personal life Shammai was a humble man devoted to truth to the extent that he could admit publicly that Jonathan ben Uziel, one of Hillel's pupils, was right and that he, the *Av Bet Din*, was wrong.[18]

In *Avot D'Rabbi Natan*[19] a wonderful elaboration is given to Shammai's teaching:

> This teaches us that if a man gives his fellow all the valuable gifts in the world but with bad grace, it is as though he had given him nothing. But he who receives his

fellow with a cheerful countenance even if he gives him nothing, it is as though he had given him all the valuable gifts in the world!

Shammai was saying that a smile is worth all the precious things in the world and it is so cheap - it costs the giver nothing.

The Mishnah and the Gemara are full of discussions and deliberations of the schools of Hillel and Shammai although between the two founders themselves only three differences of opinion are recorded. So many and so intense were the differences of opinion between the schools that at times it seemed as though Israel had two Torahs, heaven forbid! And heaven did forbid! A voice proclaimed that both were the words of the One Living God.[20]

The differences of opinion stem from different approaches to the interpretation of the Torah. Both sides were striving to arrive at the truth and both sides were motivated by the honor of the Torah and the glory of God. That is why the Mishnah,[21] when it sought an example of "an argument for the sake of heaven," a difference of opinion motivated by a search for truth and not out of personal considerations, cited the differences of opinion between Hillel and Shammai. Although they differed on points of law and interpretation, there was no personal antagonism between them. The Talmud[22] takes care to record that: "although they (Bet Shammai) forbade certain degrees of kinship in marriage and they (Bet Hillel) permitted..., the members of Bet Shammai did not refrain from taking wives from the womenfolk of Bet Hillel and vice versa."

This behavior was in the spirit of Hillel and Shammai about whom the Mishnah[23] states:

Why are the opinions of Shammai and Hillel mentioned (in a previous *mishnah*) if they were rejected (in favor of a tradition transmitted by two less important teachers)? To teach future generations that a man should not stubbornly hold on to his opinion, for (even) these "fathers of the world" did not insist on their view (when they were faced with an authentic tradition that disagreed with them)!

This extraordinary regard for truth and personal humility is also evident from the fact that on several occasions Bet Hillel were persuaded to withdraw their opinions and ruled in accordance with Bet Shammai.[24] Shammai himself set the example. Nowhere do we find that he expressed any opposition to the two important and "socially liberal" ordinances that Hillel instituted, the *prozbul* and the rule that payment for the repurchase of a house in a walled city could be executed by depositing the money in the Temple treasury (see Chapter 7).

May we merit to be as honest as these two giants and to seek and love truth as consistently as they did.

Notes

1. *Avot* 1:15
2. *Ibid*, 1:12
3. *Yoma* 77b; *Sukkah* 28a
4. *Shabbat* 30b
5. *Ibid*, 15a
6. *Ibid*, 19a
7. *Ibid*
8. *Sanhedrin* 88b
9. *Eduyot* 5:1-5
10. *Hullin* 43b/44a
11. *Avot* 1:16
12. *Sukkah* 28a
13. *Yoma* 77b; *Hullin* 107b
14. On the basis of *Bava Metzia* 87a
15. *Shabbat* 30b
16. *Avot* 2:6
17. *Eruvin* 13b
18. *Bava Batra* 134a
19. *Avot D'Rabbi Natan* 13:4
20. *Sanhedrin* 88b; *Eruvim* 13b
21. *Avot* 5:20
22. *Yevamot* 14a
23. *Eduyot* 1:4
24. *Ibid*, 1:7-9

Rabban Gamliel the Elder

רַבָּן גַּמְלִיאֵל הָיָה אוֹמֵר: עֲשֵׂה לְךָ רַב, וְהִסְתַּלֵּק מִן הַסָּפֵק, וְאַל תַּרְבֶּה לְעַשֵּׂר אֻמָדוֹת.

Rabban Gamliel (the Elder) said: "Provide yourself with a teacher and take yourself out of doubt. Do not become accustomed to giving tithes by estimation."[1]

The first thing that draws one's attention in this *mishnah* is the fact that it does not begin with the formula, "...received the tradition from..." but directly with the words, "Rabban Gamliel said." In fact, the handing down of the tradition seems to have skipped a generation for we are told in a later *mishnah*[2] that "Rabban Johanan ben Zakkai received the tradition from Hillel and Shammai."

Rabban Gamliel was the grandson of Hillel. His father, Simeon, who is only mentioned once in the Talmud,[3] had become a *Nasi* on the death of Hillel, but since Hillel lived to be 120 years old, Simeon must have been quite advanced in years when he was elected to the presidency, and it can be assumed that he did not serve many years. It is also possible that he was overshadowed by the renowned Shammai who held the position of *Av Bet Din*. This may explain why we have no record of his laws or aphorisms.

At Simeon's death, his son Gamliel, became *Nasi*. This was the period of the two great schools, Bet Hillel and Bet Shammai, and Gamliel very definitely belonged to that of Hillel. It would, therefore, be incorrect to say that he received the tradition from Hillel *and* Shammai, since he was opposed to the latter.

Another interesting feature of our *mishnah* is the appearance, for the first time, of the title, "Rabban." This is the Aramaic form of the Hebrew, *Rabbenu*, "Our Teacher," and it was later given only to the most distinguished rabbis. It is considered the highest of the rabbinical titles and, according to some authorities, was reserved for the *Nasi* of the Sanhedrin.[4] At the same time, it seems to convey a sense of affectionate regard.

In the chapters on Hillel and Shammai we have described the rivalry between the two schools which those great men founded, and how their differences of opinion made it seem as though there were two Torahs.[5] Because of the different rulings handed down, it became increasingly difficult to receive a clear, unequivocal Halachic decision on any given question. Rabban Gamliel, bearing as he did the responsibility of the *Nasi*, must have been seriously concerned with this state of affairs and with the sense of instability it created among the ordinary, unlearned people. Therefore, he advised them to adopt one scholar as their teacher and to follow that scholar's interpretations and rulings consistently. Thus, and only thus, could doubt be avoided.

The Mishnah[6] records that on one occasion Rabban Gamliel, being unsure of an *halachah* himself, turned to the Sanhedrin for advice, and that on another occasion,[7] the Master of the Temple Mount asked him for a ruling while he was standing at one of the Temple gates. The Talmud[8] also records that once Agrippa I, the king of Israel and his wife, Queen Cypros, each had their servants slaughter a Paschal Lamb and did not know which of the lambs they should use at the *Seder* ceremony. Agrippa told his servants to ask the Queen but she sent them to Rabban Gamliel.

Because of the constant discussion and argumentation between Bet Hillel and Bet Shammai, Rabban Gamliel tried to inaugurate religious rule by one man who would be the head of the Sanhedrin. He believed that this would be for the good of the community . There would be one "Chief Rabbi" who would issue authoritative rulings and thus the community would be freed of doubt.

It was this concern for clarity and precision that led Rabban Gamliel to preach the last part of his *mishnah*, "Do not become accustomed to giving tithes by estimation." The connection between this and the first aphorism is that in order to give tithes one must measure one's produce accurately in order to know how much to give. While it is true that for *Terumah*, the tithe given directly to the *kohanim*, any amount is acceptable, even one grain. The sages[9], however, ruled that one should not give less than one-sixtieth or more than one-fortieth. The First Tithe, *Maaser Rishon*, which is given to the Levites, the Second Tithe, *Maaser Sheynee*, which is to be consumed in Jerusalem, and *Maaser Ani*, the tithe for the poor which is given in the third and sixth years in place of the Second Tithe, must be one tenth of the crop measured accurately (Numbers 18:24; Deuteronomy 14:22-26, 28-29, 26:12). Rabban Gamliel was, therefore, saying that just as you should not give tithes by guesswork; so too you must not hand down an Halachik decision by guesswork; you must examine every matter to the minutest detail to be absolutely certain that your decision is the correct one.

Following the example set by his grandfather, Hillel, Rabban Gamliel also introduced new *takkanot*, ordinances, for the welfare of the community. The Torah law is, that facts can only be established "by the mouth of two witnesses," yet Rabban Gamliel ordained[10] that in the case of the *agunah*, a deserted wife, the testimony of one witness is sufficient to establish the husband's death and thus permit her to remarry. Another *takkanah* that he instituted[11] was that all names and surnames, even non-Biblical, be recorded in a *get*, a bill-of-divorce, so that the parties to the divorce should be accurately identified in the document which must, by law (Deut. 24:1), be written "for him (the husband), for her (the wife), and for the purpose of (their) divorce." In order to avoid other complications in divorce which might lead to the divorce being invalidated, Rabban Gamliel also initiated the procedure[12] that the witnesses to the divorce, who are integral to the process, must sign the actual *get* and not just merely testify that it was delivered.

Besides these procedural reforms, Rabban Gamliel instituted *takkanot*, which exhibit his deep concern for human suffering. The Mishnah[13] records that the original law was that a widow, coming to claim payment of her *ketubbah*, marriage contract, from her late husband's estate, had to take an oath before his heirs that she had not yet received any part of it. Because swearing an oath involved the pronouncement of God's name and was viewed with fear and trepidation, many women were prepared to forego what was due to them (and consequently suffer great need) rather than swear the oath. Rabban Gamliel did away with this requirement, and the widow could collect by vowing - a much less serious process than swearing an oath - that she had not yet received any payment.

Not only did Rabban Gamliel try to improve society through legislation, but he also realized the tremendous prestige that went with the office of *Nasi* and used it by setting an example which the people followed willingly. The Talmud[14] records:

> Earlier, burying the dead was more difficult for the relatives than the death of their loved one itself because of the high cost of the shrouds that social convention and competition forced them to buy; so much so, that people would just leave their dead (without burial) and run away! Until Rabban Gamliel came and treated himself lightly and was buried in simple linen shrouds. After that, everybody buried their dead in linen shrouds.

Some commentators say that Rabban Gamliel buried one of his close relatives in simple shrouds, while others say that he gave instructions that he himself was to be buried so. (In

Tosafot the latter explanation is preferred.)

In ancient times, a number of *berakhot*, benedictions of comfort, used to be recited at the home of the mourners during the *shivah* period and the Talmud[15] tells us that a special benediction was instituted in honor of Rabban Gamliel to commemorate the wonderful example he set which relieved a shameful social situation.

It is also possible to interpret Rabban Gamliel's aphorism as being directed to teachers themselves: "Make yourself a teacher and remove all doubt from your teaching," i.e., prepare your lessons thoroughly so as to remove any doubt in the minds of your students.

In order to declare a new month, witnesses would come to the Sanhedrin in Jerusalem to testify that they had seen the first crescent of the new moon. On the basis of this testimony the court would declare that day the first of the month, Rosh Hodesh, and this would establish the dates of the festivals during that month. Fixing the months was thus exceedingly important and it was the exclusive province of the Sanhedrin in Jerusalem. In order to encourage people who had seen the moon's first crescent to come to Jerusalem and deliver their testimony, Rabban Gamliel permitted[16] them to walk out of the city for 2,000 cubits in each direction on the Sabbath as though they were dwellers in the city, although according to the strict law they would be denied this because they had arrived in the city on Shabbat from a distance of more than 2,000 cubits.

In Rabban Gamliel's time inter-faith relations, as we would call them today, became a pressing issue. There was a great deal of contact with the Romans and many of the aristocrats were showing an interest in Judaism. Furthermore, Eretz Israel had a considerable non-Jewish population and this period also witnessed the rise of Christianity. Rabban Gamliel is credited with a number of rulings in this area which appear in the sources anonymously.[17] He ruled[18] that the poor must be provided for, regardless of their faith; that the non-Jewish sick should be visited just as the Jewish sick, and that non-Jews should be given a decent burial. He even went so far as to rule that the non-Jewish poor had the right to take *leket, shikhah* and *peah*, the gleanings, forgotten sheaves and corners of the field that the Jewish farmer is required to leave for the poor (Leviticus 19:9-10). All these rulings were issued to improve relations with the non-Jews.

It was fortunate that for some years of Rabban Gamliel's presidency, that Eretz Israel was ruled by Agrippa I, the grandson of Herod and Marriamne, the Hasmonean princess. Agrippa had been educated in Rome and was a friend of the emperors, Caligula and Claudius. In fact he had been instrumental in the latter's elevation to the emperorship. Although Agrippa had led a dissipated life in his youth, when he ascended the throne he changed his ways and became, together with his wife, Cypros, a very pious Jew. He was a benevolent monarch and made great efforts to please all his subjects, Jews and non-Jews alike. He was exceedingly considerate as far as the Jewish religion was concerned and went out of his way to show his regard for the rabbis. He released the inhabitants of Jerusalem from taxes and rebuilt the walls of the city. For the non-Jewish towns he built theaters and public buildings. Because of his knowledge of Rome and his good connections with the governing circles there, he was able to preserve the delicate balance needed to keep the peace. Rabban Gamliel must have received royal approval and encouragement in the various ordinances he enacted.

Perhaps the best known of Rabban Gamliel's rulings[19] is the one quoted in the Passover Haggadah which we recite on the *Seder* night: "Rabban Gamliel used to say, 'Whoever does not mention these three things on the night of Passover has not fulfilled his duty: *Pesah* (the Paschal Lamb), *Matzah*, and *Maror* (Bitter Herbs).' In his times the Temple was still standing and eating the Paschal Lamb was the central part of the festive meal. The celebrants had to touch the Paschal Lamb and recite the reasons for its sacrifice and consumption. Today we only touch the *matzah* and the *maror* and explain their significance. It is not enough just to mention these things; The Jew must actually touch them in order to feel the idea of the slavery in Egypt, physically. Only then will we appreciate the grace of the Almighty in delivering us from it and only then can he truly praise Him.

The Talmud states[20] that when Rabban Gamliel died the glory of the Torah ceased and purity and self-denial perished.

Notes

1. *Avot* 1:6
2. *Ibid05, 2:9*
3. *Shabbat* 15a
4. *Letter of Sherira Gaon*; see *Arukh, s.v. Abbaye*
5. *Sanhedrin* 88b
6. *Peah* 2:6
7. *Orlah* 2:12
8. *Pesahim* 88b
9. *Shabbat* 17b; *Terumot* 4:3
10. *Yevamot* 115a-122a
11. *Gittin* 34b
12. *Ibid*
13. *Ibid*
14. *Moed Katan* 27b
15. *Ketubbot* 8b
16. *Rosh Hashanah* 23G
17. J:H:Weiss, *Dor Dor Ve-Dorshav*, Chapter 20
18. *Tosefta; Gittin* 61a-59b
19. *Pesahim* 116a/b
20. *Sotah*, 49a

Simeon ben Gamliel

שִׁמְעוֹן בְּנוֹ אוֹמֵר: כָּל יָמַי גָּדַלְתִּי בֵּין הַחֲכָמִים וְלֹא מָצָאתִי לַגּוּף
טוֹב מִשְּׁתִיקָה, וְלֹא הַמִּדְרָשׁ עִקָּר אֶלָּא הַמַּעֲשֶׂה, וְכָל הַמַּרְבֶּה
דְּבָרִים מֵבִיא חֵטְא.

*Simeon his son used to say:"All my life I have grown up
among the sages and I have not discovered anything better
for a person (*guf*) than silence; it is not the learning (or
exposition) that is the most important thing but rather the
doing (performance) and whoever talks a great deal brings
sin."*[1]

The identity of Simeon, the author of this *mishnah*, is not
absolutely clear since he is only identified with the description,
"his son." The question is, whose son was he?

It can be argued[2] that this Simeon who is mentioned only
once in the Talmud was the son of Hillel the Elder.[3] Perhaps it
is the silence which he advocates in the *mishnah* that accounts
for the paucity of references to him. We know that Simeon
succeeded his father Hillel as *Nasi* and it is strange that he is not
mentioned in Avot in the chain of tradition. According to this
theory we would have to say that our *mishnah* has been
misplaced and should appear before that of Rabban Gamliel
who was this Simeon's son. Most commentators, however, feel
that the Simeon of our *mishnah* was the son of Rabban Gamliel
and the great-grandson of Hillel. "His son," coming
immediately after Rabban Gamliel, naturally refers to him.

Simeon succeeded his father, Rabban Gamliel, to the
presidency of the Sanhedrin. He is referred to in this *mishnah*

without the title Rabban, because he made these statements before he was elevated to that important position. Indeed, the first part of the *mishnah* can be taken as being directed to students. Nothing is better than silence; first listen and absorb what the teacher is saying; do not ask questions until you have learnt a great deal. With learning, you will yourself realize the answers to many of your questions and in the course of his teaching your instructor may very well deal with some of the points that you want to raise.

It is, however, also possible to interpret Rabban Simeon's dictum on a wider basis. He did not use the Hebrew word, *adam*, which is generally used for a person but the term *guf*, which actually means "body", and it may very well be that he is directing his wise advice to the Sanhedrin *as a body*.

With the death of King Agrippa I and Rabban Gamliel, Simeon's father, the situation of the Jews in Eretz Israel deteriorated rapidly. The greed and cruelty of the Roman procurators knew no limits and they oppressed the Jews to such an extent that the rule of Albinus was considered as benevolent when compared to that of the later Florus.[4] Spies were everywhere - in the market places and even in the *yeshivot*, and any statement even slightly critical of the regime was immediately reported to the authorities and brought its utterer instant punishment, often death.

Like his great-grandfather and his father before him, Rabban Simeon loved and pursued peace, but even he could not contain himself at the excesses of the Romans and, sad to say, the Jews who collaborated with them. Bands of robbers preyed on the populace with immunity as long as they shared their spoil with Florus, the avaricious Roman govenor.[5] This was the period before the great revolt against Rome and talk of rebellion was rife. No wonder, then, that the *Nasi* advised his colleagues: "Nothing is better for this body (the Sanhedrin) than silence!" At a later date, after the destruction of the Temple, Rabbi Simeon bar Yohai had to flee for his life because of an indiscreet remark (see Chapter 19).

Even among the top echelons of those planning the revolt against Rome, there were men whose integrity was suspect. A good example of this is the case of Joseph ben Mattityahu, the *Kohain* who was appointed commander of the rebel forces in the Galilee. Later, it was felt that he was untrustworthy and the council decided to recall him to Jerusalem and dismiss him.[6] Rabban Simeon's advice of silence was apparently not heeded, and Joseph's friends were able to forewarn him of the steps that were to be taken against him with the result that he was able to frustrate the will of the supreme council. This Joseph sold out to the Romans and became a member of Vespasian's household,[7] taking the family name of the Flavians and was later known as Flavius Josephus. He was the author of *The Antiquities of the Jews*, a complete history of the Jewish people up to his time, and *The Wars of the Jews*, an account of the struggle against Rome. These books, like his others, were written in Greek.

Although Josephus knew that Rabban Simeon had distrusted him and had wanted his dismissal, he nevertheless praises Rabban Simeon in his books as a worthy *Nasi* of the Sanhedrin and as a wise and prudent leader of the nation.[8] It is interesting to note that Rabban Simeon was quite justified in his distrust of Josephus as the later events clearly proved.

It is not the learning that is the most important thing but the doing.

Rabban Simeon, as *Nasi* of the Sanhedrin, believed that "actions speak louder than words," and he practiced what he preached. Although the times were very difficult and the country was in a state of confusion, the service at the Temple continued and Rabban Simeon enacted laws which, at first glance, might seem to be contrary to Torah law.

The Bible states that a woman who has given birth must bring at least two doves as a sacrifice to the Temple (Leviticus

12:8). In Rabban Simeon's time the price of doves became exorbitant, no doubt because of the turbulent state of the country. People could not afford the high price and thus ceased to bring the required sacrifices. Rabban Simeon decreed that a woman could offer one pair of doves for as many as five births and the price of doves fell overnight.[9]

Another example of Rabban Simeon's concern for the public welfare is his statement that the court sould not intercalate a year or take any public action unless it is certain that the majority of the community will be able to accept it.[10]

Rabban Simeon was not an aloof person and enjoyed taking part in festivities connected with *mitzvot*. One of the important *mitzvot* over which the Sadducees had disagreed with the Pharisees was the "Drawing of Water" ceremony during the Sukkot festival in which water was poured over the altar in the Temple. Hillel the Elder had so loved this ceremony that he declared,[11] "If I am here, everybody is here." and the Mishnah tells us that "he who has not seen the Water Drawing ceremony, has never seen joy!"[11]   Rabban Simeon's contribution to the festivities was, that he juggled eight flaming torches for the entertainment of the masses, gathered at the celebration.

In addition to his spiritual and judicial duties, Rabban Simeon was also one of the leaders of the revolt against Rome. The situation had become intolerable. Even the moderate elements became involved in the struggle against the world's mightiest power, a struggle which ultimately led to the destruction of the Second Temple and the long exile that followed. Rabban Simeon's participation in planning the revolt was discovered by the Roman authorities and he, together with Ishmail ben Elisha, the High Priest, were condemned to death and executed.[12] In the *piyyut*, *Eleh Ezkerah* ("These Do I Remember"), which forms a central part of the Yom Kippur synagogue service, they are the first of the ten martyrs whose deaths are described. The *paytan*, with the privilege of poetic licence, describes the martyrdom as though it all happened at one time, although, historically, the martyrs belonged to different generations. In the *piyyut*, which is based on midrashic material, the Roman oppressor justifies his cruelty by claiming that the Jews are liable to the death penalty because the brothers kidnapped and sold Joseph (Genesis 37:27) and kidnapping is a capital offence. The brothers had not paid for their crime, therefore, the rabbis, as heirs, were obliged to die in their place. This is, of course, a poetic expression; the historical truth is that the Romans were trying to stamp out the revolt by destroying the national leadership.

In the Talmud[13] we are told that Samuel Ha-Katan ("The Small") prophesied before his own death that Simeon and Ishmael would die by the sword, that the other sages would be killed in different ways and that the Jewish people would suffer horrible trials and tribulations.

The Talmud[14] also records a heart-rending conversation between these two martyrs before their execution:

On hearing the death sentence, Ishmael, the High Priest, began to weep and Rabban Simeon tried to comfort him. "Why do you weep?" he asked, "Two steps more and you will be in the bosom of the righteous." "It is not because we are going to be killed," answered Ishmael, "but because we are to die in the same fashion (i.e. by the sword) as murderers and Sabbath desecrators."

"Perhaps," suggested Rabban Simeon, "you were once eating or resting when a woman came to ask a question about her period or as to whether she was ritually pure and your servant told her that he could not disturb you, and that she should return later. The Torah says: 'You shall not mistreat any widow or orphan. If you do mistreat them, I will heed their complaint... and I will put you to the sword...' (Exodus 22: 21-23)."

This account is a remarkable example of rabbinic piety. Rabban Simeon and Rabbi Ishmael did not question the

Almighty's justice - they justified the decree. The method in which the decree was to be executed is what bothered Ishmael - he acknowledged that the Almighty is just in even the smallest detail.

The *paytan* of *Eleh Ezkerah* adds another dimension to the tragic story. Rabban Simeon begged the executioner to execute him first so that he should not have to witness the death of Ishmael, the *Kohen Gadol* who was the intermediary between God and Israel. Ishmael, on the other hand, demanded that he be the first to be executed so that he should not see the death of the *Nasi*, who was a direct descendant of King David. Finally, they drew lots and Rabban Simeon was executed first.

Perhaps Rabban Simeon was endowed with unconscious prophecy when he said in our *mishnah*, "Whoever talks a great deal brings sin." Somebody must have been indiscreet and because of too much talk these two giants of Jewish history were apprehended and put to death.

The Talmud[15] continues the account of the executions:

When the news of the execution of Rabban Simeon and Rabbi Ishmael reached Rabbi Akiva and Rabbi Judah ben Bava, they arose, donned sackcloth and tore their garments and they announced: "Oh, our bretheren Israel! If good news were to come into the world, the first to receive it would have been Rabban Simeon and Rabbi Ishmael. It is clear to Him, at whose word the world came into being, that great suffering is about to come into the world and therefore these two righteous men have been removed from it as it is written, "The righteous man perishes and no one takes it to heart and goodly men die and no one understands that the righteous man is taken away before the evil comes. He shall enter into peace, they shall rest on their beds, each one who walks upright' (Isaiah 57:1-2)."

Notes

1. *Avot* 1:17
2. *Seder Ha-Dorot*
3. *Shabbat* 15a
4. Josephus, *Antiquities* 20:11
5. *Ibid*
6. *The Life of Josephus*, Ch. 38
7. *Ibid*, Ch.74-75
8. *Ibid*, Ch.38
9. *Keritot*, 8a
10. *Avodah Zarah* 36a
11. *Sukkah* , 53a
12. *Midrash Rabbah, Lamentations* 2:4
13. *Sotah* 48b; *Sanhedrin* 11a
14. *Semahot* Ch. 8. According to another reading it was Rabban Simeon who wept. This is also the reading in the version that appears in *Avot d' Rabbi Natan.* 32b-33a
15. *Semahot* Ch. 8

Rabban Gamliel of Yavneh

Rabbi Judah said in the name of Rabban Gamliel: "The Torah states, 'And He will give you compassion and He will be compassionate to you and increase you' (Deuteronomy 13:18). Let this be a slogan for you: As long as you are merciful, the All-Merciful will have mercy on you!"[1]

This aphorism is also cited in the Jerusalem Talmud[2] but in the Babylonian Talmud[3] it appears in a slightly different form: Rabban Gamliel the son of Rabbi (i.e. Rabbi Judah the Nasi) said, "And He will give you..." he who is merciful to others (literally: the creatures), is shown mercy from heaven; but he who is not merciful to others is not shown mercy from heaven." Besides the slight diference in formulation, the Babylonian Talmud ascribes the aphorism to Rabban Gamliel III who was the son of Rabbi Judah the Nasi, whereas in the Tosefta and the Jerusalem Talmud it is Rabbi Judah the Nasi who quotes Rabban Gamliel who is presumably Rabban Gamliel II of Yavneh who was his grandfather. It can thus be assumed that the author was Rabban Gamliel of Yavneh and, indeed, the Rosh, in his review of the section in the Babylonian Talmud,[3] quotes the aphorism in the name of Rabban Gamliel without any other description and when the name Rabban Gamliel appears without qualification it always refers to Rabban Gamliel of Yavneh.

It is indeed surprising that Rabbi Judah the Nasi did not see fit to include any of his grandfather's sayings in Avot: after all, Rabban Gamliel was the president of the Sanhedrin in Yavneh and one of the leading sages of all times. Even more surprising is the fact that Rabban Gamliel's aphorism cited at the beginning of this chapter is quoted by Rabbi Judah himself and even more surprising still is the fact that Rabbi Judah suffered the consequences of ignoring his grandfather's advice.[4] He became seriously ill because he did not show compassion and only recovered when he took mercy on a nest of weasels (see Chapter 15). It should also be remembered that Rabban Gamliel of Yavneh is mentioned more than two hundred times in the Talmud. Yet he is not mentioned in Avot, and what more fitting an aphorism could there be for Avot than "As long as you are merciful, the All-Merciful will have mercy on you!?"

Rabban Gamliel lived during the period of the destruction of the Second Temple. The Talmud[5] records that he was sentenced to death by the Roman authorities and that a certain dignitary (presumably a Roman officer) warned him of this sentence, and he managed to escape and go into hiding. This dignitary came into the study-hall and called out, "the man with the long nose is wanted!" Rabban Gamliel understood the hint "The man with the long nose" is interpreted to mean "The outstanding man" . This expression was necessary because the Roman was afraid for his own life. Later, the dignitary secretly visited Rabban Gamliel in his hiding place and said to him, "Now that I saved you, can you guarantee me a place in the World-to-Come?"

Rabban Gamliel swore an oath that he would have such a place and the Roman threw himself off a roof and died. At that time a voice came from heaven and announced that he did receive a place in the World-to-Come.

Rabban Johanan ben Zakkai[6] secured a pardon for Rabban Gamliel from the Roman commander, Vespasian (see Chapter 16) and subsequently Rabban Gamliel took his place among the scholars at Yavneh, where, some ten years after the destruction of the Temple, he was appointed *Nasi*.

In his conduct as president of the Sanhedrin, Rabban Gamliel was exceedingly strict and would brook no opposition to his authority, but in his personal life and in his dealings with the unlearned and simple folk he was very kind and considerate. It is recorded[7] that when he loaned his tenant-farmers seed for the planting season, he always took repayment at the lower price irrespective of whether the price of seed had increased or decreased. On one occasion[8] when the child of a neighbor died, he heard the mother weeping at night and he too wept in sympathy the whole night "until his eyelashes fell out." He was very attached to his slave, Tabi, and although the *Halakhah* does not allow non-Jewish slaves to be freed, Rabban Gamliel made every effort to find an halakhic loophole so as to set him free. When Tabi died, Rabban Gamliel accepted condolences for him although the *Halakhah* states that one should not accept condolences for a slave. He felt that "my slave was not like other slaves - he was a good man!"[9] In his attitude to non-Jews in general he was considerate. He ruled[10] that it is forbidden to cheat them because that constitutes a desecration of God's name.

In his official activities as *Nasi* of the Sanhedrin, however, Rabban Gamliel revealed a completely different side of his character. He was entirely authoritarian and seemed to believe that the academy and the Sanhedrin could only fulfil their mission and lead the nation if the authority of the presidency was absolute. To this end he demanded of his colleagues complete obedience. It is almost as though he identified the Sanhedrin with its president.

This attitude was handed down in the family. When Rabbi Judah the Nasi was about to depart this world[11] he instructed his own son, Rabban Gamliel III, "Conduct your presidency with men of high standing and cast bile among the students," and it can be assumed that this was advice which was transmitted from *Nasi to Nasi.*

One of the important functions of the Sanhedrin was to fix the calendar particularly with regards to intercalation. In order to adjust the lunar cycle to the solar cycle (which is slightly longer) it is necessary to add an extra month. Nowadays, this is done by a fixed mathematical-astronomical formula which intercalates a Second Adar into certain years of the cycle. Since the months are fixed on a lunar basis and the festivals are on specific dates in the months, if there were no such intercalation the festivals would "wander" and Passover, which is called in the Bible "The Festival of Spring," would move into other seasons because the seasons depend on the solar cycle and not the lunar. In the times of the Sanhedrin the intercalation was also enacted according to agricultural criteria and the Sanhedrin had to decide each year whether to intercalate or not. Rabban Gamliel insisted on the rule, "The year can be intercalated only if the *Nasi* so approves," and on one occasion,[12] when he was in Syria on official business and delayed his return, the question of whether to intercalate became urgent. Because of its diffidence vis-a-vis Rabbi Gamliel, the Sanhedrin intercalated "on condition that the *Nasi* will so approve." Fortunately, when he returned, Rabban Gamliel expressed his agreement.

There is also a rule that "The year can be intercalated only by the invited (scholars)."[13] Rabban Gamliel once invited seven of the sages to join him in the discussion and the ceremony of intercalation, but when he arrived at the place appointed for the meeting he found eight scholars there. He insisted that "he who is here uninvited must leave!" Samuel Ha-Katan ("The Small"), an outstandingly pious man, said, "I am here uninvited but I did not come to take part in the ceremony but only to study practical *Halakhah*." Rabban Gamliel told him, "Sit, my son. All the years could be intercalated by you but the law is that you must be invited." The Talmud remarks that it was one of the other sages who had come uninvited and that Samuel Ha-Katan had taken the blame on himself in order to prevent the uninvited sage from being embarassed. It should be pointed out that Samuel Ha-Katan was one of Rabban Gamliel's favorite colleagues.

Intercalation was not the only function of the Sanhedrin with regards to the calendar. Another of its prerogatives was the fixing of the months themselves. This function of the Sanhedrin was crucial because by it the dates of the festivals were fixed. Rabban Gamliel was adamant that his was the absolute authority to decide on this matter and that all must follow his decision. This is very understandable for if individual sages were allowed to disagree, chaos would ensue in the religious life of the nation. The beginning of the month *Rosh Hodesh* was fixed by the court on the basis of the testimony of two witnesses who had seen the first crescent of the new moon. If there were no such witnesses on the twenty-ninth day after the previous *Rosh Hodesh*, the thirtieth day automatically became the next *Rosh Hodesh*. The witnesses were examined by the court to make sure that what they claimed to have seen was possible according to the laws of astronomy. Rabban Gamliel even had diagrams of the moon in all its phases throughout the year and insisted that the witnesses indicate on them what they had seen.[14]

On one occasion[15] Rabbi Joshua disagreed with Rabban Gamliel's decision with regards to *Rosh Hodesh* Tishre. He was convinced that the witnesses, whose testimony Rabban Gamliel had accepted, were false or mistaken witnesses because the facts as they had described them were impossible. Other important members of the Sanhedrin agreed with Rabbi Joshua but Rabban Gamliel refused to change his decision. He insisted that Rabbi Joshua appear before him with his staff and his money on the day which, according to Rabbi Joshua's reckoning, was Yom Kippur. Rabbi Haninah and Rabbi Akiva agreed that Rabban Gamliel had erred in his decision but they advised Rabbi Joshua to acquiesce on the grounds that once the decision is taken it must be honored. Rabbi Joshua took their advice and when he appeared before Rabban Gamliel, the latter kissed him on his head and said, "Come in peace, my teacher and my pupil! My teacher in wisdom and my pupil in that you accepted my decision!"[14]

Rabbi Joshua was one of the most respected members of the

Sanhedrin and although this incident ended amicably, a
further confrontation was in the offing. This time it was over
the question of whether the evening prayers *ma'ariv* are
obligatory. All agree that the morning *shaharit* and afternoon
minhah prayers are obligatory because they stand in place of
the morning and afternoon sacrifices that were offered in the
Temple; the evening service is problematic - some sages felt
that it too is compulsory while others disagreed and ruled that
its recitation was voluntary. The fact that Daniel is reported to
have prayed three times a day (Daniel 6:11) is no proof, since he
may have recited the evening prayers voluntarily.

A student[16] Rabbi Simeon bar Yohai, according to the
Talmud (see chap.19) asked Rabbi Joshua for his opinion on
this matter and he replied that the evening service is voluntary.
The student then went and asked Rabban Gamliel the same
question. He gave the opposite opinion. "But," said the
student, "Rabbi Joshua said it is voluntary!" Rabban Gamliel
told him to wait until the scholars assemble in the study-hall.
When the court assembled on the following day. the student at
Rabban Gamliel's instigation, asked the question: "Is *ma'ariv*
obligatory or voluntary?" Rabban Gamliel answered,
"Obligatory! Does anybody disagree?" Rabbi Joshua
answered, "No." "But I have been told that you rule it is
voluntary. Joshua, stand on your feet so that your colleagues
can testify against you!" Rabbi Joshua stood up and said, "If I
were alive and he (the student) was dead, the living can deny the
dead. But both he and I are alive, how can the living deny the
living?!"

Rabban Gamliel remained seated and continued his lecture
leaving Rabbi Joshua standing. The indignity which was thus
being heaped on Rabbi Joshua was too much for the rest of the
sages to bear and they called out to Hutzpit the Translator
who was repeating on Rabban Gamliel's softly spoken words
to the assembly in a loud voice, to stop. He did. The sages then
said, "How long is Rabban Gamliel going to be allowed to

insult Rabbi Joshua? He insulted him over Yom Kippur; he insulted him over Rabbi Zadok's firstling calf;[17] and now he has done it again! Come, let us depose him!"

The harassment that Rabbi Joshua suffered at the hands of Rabban Gamliel was "the straw that broke the camel's back." Rabban Gamliel had been involved in a serious dispute with the respected Rabbi Akiva[18] and had also excommunicated his own brother-in-law, Rabbi Eliezer ben Hyrcanus because he had refused to accept a decision of the Sanhedrin.[19] Rabban Gamliel had also limited admission to the academy very severely. He had ruled[20] that only those "whose interior (inner character) corresponds to their exterior attitude" were to be allowed in and to this purpose had posted a guard at the entrance to the study-hall. Obviously, the guard could not possibly know whether the applicants fitted Rabban Gamliel's criterion and thus the onus fell on the applicants themselves. Those who could not agree with Rabban Gamliel's concept of the manner in which the academy was to be conducted stayed away of their own accord. Others felt that since Rabban Gamliel was the *Nasi* he was to be obeyed right or wrong. This latter attitude was summed up by Rabbi Johanan ben Nuri[21] who rejected a well-based objection of Rabbi Joshua against Rabban Gamliel in another matter with the words; "The body the Sanhedrin must follow the head the *Nasi* ." Between these two extremes there was a third group of sages, who followed Rabban Gamliel's rulings, because he was *Nasi*, but disagreed with him.

The Talmud records the discussion that took place to find a replacement for Rabban Gamliel.[16] The obvious candidate was Rabbi Joshua, but the idea was rejected because he had been the person on whose account Rabban Gamliel had been deposed. Rabbi Akiva's candidacy was not accepted because of his genealogy; he was a descendant of prosylites. Ultimately, the position was offered to Rabbi Eleazar ben Azariah who was an outstanding scholar of distinguished lineage, being the tenth generation from Ezra. His only drawback was his age - he was eighteen years old. Rabbi Eleazar went to consult his wife who advised him to refuse because ultimately, she felt, Rabban Gamliel would be forgiven and restored as *Nasi*. Rabbi Eleazar ignored his wife's advice and accepted the appointment on the grounds that "it is better to drink from an exquisite goblet even if it is later broken." When his wife objected that he was too young to command the respect appropriate for the *Nasi*, a miracle occurred and his hair turned white.

To Rabban Gamliel's credit it must be said that he continued to attend the academy as an ordinary member and took part in its deliberations.[16] The influx of large numbers of new students into the academy under the new regime, caused Rabban Gamliel a great deal of soul-searching. "Did I, Heaven forbid, prevent the study of Torah?" The Talmud records that he dreamt a reassuring dream in which he was shown that the new students were not fit to attend the academy; but the Talmud remarks that it was not true and that he was only given the dream in order to put his mind at ease.

Finally, Rabban Gamliel visited Rabbi Joshua to apologise.[16] When he came into Rabbi Joshua's house he saw that the walls were black with soot, for Rabbi Joshua earned his meagre living as a charcoal-maker (or, according to other versions, as a needle-maker). Rabban Gamliel said in amazement, "I see that you are a charcoal-maker!" "Woe to the generation of which you are a leader," answered Rabbi Joshua, "for you have no understanding of the trials of the sages or of how they live!" At first Rabbi Joshua refused to accept the apology and only relented when Rabban Gamliel begged him, "Forgive me for my father's sake!" Rabbi Joshua went to the academy to try and have Rabban Gamliel reinstated but met with some opposition. Rabbi Akiva said, "Rabbi Joshua, you have been conciliated and we did the whole thing because of you!" But the problem of Rabbi Eleazar remained - what could be done with him? Ultimately, he was given an official appointment in the Sanhedrin (*Av Bet Din*, according to some commentators) and given the privilege of preaching on one Sabbath or week every month while Rabban Gamliel had the other three.

The story of Rabban Gamliel's deposition as presented in the Talmud provides some serious problems. Firstly, why did Rabbi Joshua explicitly say that he did not disagree with Rabban Gamliel's opinion when he had told the student that *ma'ariv* was voluntary? Furthermore, at the very end of the account the Talmud adds,[16] "And that student was Rabbi Simeon bar Yohai." If the identity of the student is significant, why did not the Talmud include it in the story itself and tell us that Simeon bar Yohai asked the question? It has been suggested that the whole incident was, in fact, a tragic mistake.

The Talmud,[22] in another place, discusses the question of whether one must interrupt Torah study in order to recite the *Shema* and say one's prayers. After all, Torah study is a *mitzvah* and the rule is that when one is engaged in performing a *mitzvah* one is not obligated to perform other *mitzvot*. The conclusion of the Talmud is that one must interrupt Torah learning for *Shema* and for prayer, but that people like Rabbi Simeon bar Yohai and his companions, whose learning is their only occupation, they need not stop their studies in order to pray. Thus, when Rabbi Joshua was asked by Rabbi Simeon bar Yohai, he answered that *ma'ariv* is voluntary and he meant this for Rabbi Simeon bar Yohai only. When he agreed in the academy that *ma'ariv* was compulsory he was referring to ordinary people. Thus the Talmud remarks, laconically, that the student was Simeon bar Yohai and is hinting that the whole uproar was unnecessary.

Be that as it may, "that day" of Rabban Gamliel's deposition was a traumatic event in Talmudic history and was remembered for generations. Might it be possible that Rabbi Judah the Nasi left his grandfather out of Avot in order not to arouse historical memories of "that day" and thus remind his colleagues that it is possible to overthrow even a *Nasi* of Hillel's genealogy ?

Rabban Gamliel was, however, a giant in his generation and must have been motivated by more than a desire to maintain or increase his own personal glory. His attitude toward the unlearned populace was forgiving because by nature he was a sympathetic person and forgave them their ignorance. But, he realized that the authority of the academy and the Sanhedrin was crucial for the survival of Judaism and that there must be discipline, otherwise the Torah would be splintered into many Torahs. If the older, respected members of the academy, like Rabbi Joshua, Rabbi Akiva and Rabbi Eliezer ben Hyrcanus, did not show that discipline, how could he demand it from the younger members? No doubt he went too far in his strictures towards these men and should have rather brought them to participate more in the formal leadership but his motives were surely pure.

Indeed, many of the pillars of Judaism today, such as the texts of the prayers and the procedure of the *Seder* on the night of Passover, were established and formulated under his guidance.

Notes

1. *Tosefta, Bava Kama* 9:11
2. *TJ Bava Kama* 8:7
3. *Shabbat* 151b
4. *Bava Metzia* 85a
5. *Ta'anit* 29a
6. *Gittin* 56b
7. *Bava Metzia* 74b
8. *Sanhedrin* 104b
9. *Berakhot* 16b
10. *TJ Bava Kama* 4:3
11. *Ketubbat* 103b
12. *Sanhedrin* 11a
13. *Ibid*
14. *Rosh Ha-Shanah* 24a
15. *Ibid*, 25a
16. *Berakhot* 27b-28a
17. *Bekoroth* 36a
18. *Rosh Ha-Shanah* 21b
19. *Bava Metzia* 59b
20. *Berakhot* 28a
21. *Eruvin* 41a
22. *Shabbat* 11a; I am indebted to HaRav HaGaon, Rabbi Abrahan Kroll for this insight.

Rabban Simeon ben Gamliel of Yavneh

רַבָּן שִׁמְעוֹן בֶּן גַּמְלִיאֵל אוֹמֵר: עַל שְׁלשָׁה דְבָרִים הָעוֹלָם קַיָּם:
עַל הַדִּין וְעַל הָאֱמֶת וְעַל הַשָּׁלוֹם, שֶׁנֶּאֱמַר: אֱמֶת וּמִשְׁפַּט שָׁלוֹם
שִׁפְטוּ בְּשַׁעֲרֵיכֶם:

> *Rabbi Simeon ben Gamliel II, of Yavneh said: "On three
> things the world exists: on truth, on justice, on peace; as it is
> written, 'You shall administer justice, truth and peace in
> your gates' (Zechariah 8:16)."*[1]

There were two sages called Simeon ben Gamliel; the first was
the great grandson of Hillel and he was the first of the ten
martyrs executed by the Romans[2] (see Chapter 11). The author
of our *mishnah* was this Rabban Simeon's grandson and the
father of Rabbi Judah the Nasi, the redactor of the Mishnah.
Rabbi Judah, thus closes the first chapter of Avot with an
aphorism of his father.

The second aphorism in chapter I is that of Simeon the
Tzaddik, "The world stands on three things: Torah, divine
worship, and the practice of charity."[3] At first glance, there
would appear to be some duplication, between Rabban
Simeon's statement and that of Simeon the Tzaddik.

The accepted explanation is that Simeon the Tzaddik was
referring to the creation of the world, while Simeon ben Gamliel
is referring to the continued existence of the world and is
teaching us that only truth and justice can ensure the continued
peace of human existence.

However, to whom was Rabban Simeon addressing his
remark? Was it to the general populace or was it to the judges?

Surely, the *Halakhah* is perfectly clear concerning the administration of justice and provides detailed rules and regulations regarding witnesses, claims, and how to reach a decision. What then was Rabban Simeon actually saying?

It is possible that Rabban Simeon was addressing his fellow judges but with regards to litigation involving Jews and non-Jews. He was also stressing that in such cases the courts must be just and give the non-Jew all his rights although that was certainly not the case when non-Jewish courts dealt with such cases. There, the Jew was always at a considerable disadvantage. Rabban Simeon was a strong advocate of the equality of the Jew and the non-Jew before the law. He was a persistent protector of the rights of non-Jews; he ruled[4] that just as it is a religious duty to redeem a fellow Jew, who had been taken into slavery, so too should one redeem a non-Jewish slave who was taken captive and held for ransom. He also ruled[5] that when one is a partner in a field, the produce must be divided in the presence of all the partners - Jews or non-Jews - to make it absolutely clear that the division is just. Rabban Simeon even considered a Sefer Torah written by a non-Jew to be *kosher* as long as the parchment was tanned for the specific purpose of making a Sefer Torah and it was written properly.[6] His attitude toward the *Kutim*, the Samaritans, was also more favorable than that of his colleagues; he considered them to be Jews for all purposes[7] and went so far as to say that the commandments which they observe, they observe better than Jews.[8]

It would appear that Rabban Simeon ben Gamliel was trying to find a way to bring peace to the strife-torn country. He felt that if the Jews showed true friendship to the non-Jews and practiced equal justice towards them, they would perhaps change their attitude toward the Jews and peace would reign in the land. Rabban Simeon was entrusted with the leadership of the Jewish people in an extremely turbulent period. Roman oppression increased during and after the Bar Kochba revolt and he had to steer the Jewish ship of state into a safe harbor. Even in his youth, times had not been much better. He was well aware of that, as is clear from his statement: "In my father's house (academy) there were one thousand students; five hundred studied Torah and five hundred studied Greek, for my father was on very good terms with the Roman governor. Yet nothing remained of all of them except a cousin in Asia and myself."[9]

Rabban Simeon had enormous respect for his father: "All my life I attended my father but I did not show him even one-hundredth of the honor Esau showed Isaac. For I used to attend my father in ordinary clothes and go out into the street in fresh clothing but Esau used to attend Isaac in royal robes, for he said, 'Only royal garments are fitting for my father's honor!'[10]

Another indication of Rabban Simeon's evaluation of his own period can be found in a remark he made during a discussion of the authorship of *Megillat Ta'anit*. The Talmud[11] states that Hanania ben Hezekiah and his group, "who cherished the troubles," wrote this book which lists the happy days on which mournful activities, such as eulogizing the dead and fasting, are forbidden. On this, Rabban Simeon remarked, "We too cherish the troubles but what can we do? They are so many that were we to start to write them down we would never finish!"

He described[12] the fall of Betar in the Bar Kochba rebellion in the following terms: "There were four hundred synagogues in Betar and four hundred teachers who each had four hundred students. When the enemy prevailed and captured them, they were all wrapped in their scrolls and burned!" Yet, he still hoped to find a way to live in peace with the Romans.

In his love of peace, Rabban Simeon was prepared to forego the respect due to him as *Nasi*. It is recorded[13] that a man took an oath to have nothing to do with his wife unless she spat on Rabban Simeon. Apparently, this man resented his wife's piety and the honor she showed the sages. The poor woman had no choice and spat on Rabban Simeon's cloak; although this was a grievous insult, he forgave in the cause of peace (see Chapter 21 for a similar incident involving Rabbi Meir). He summed up his attitude to the sanctity of the family in a most powerful aphorism: "He who brings peace into his household is considered by Scripture to have made peace for every individual in Israel, each and every one of them; but he who causes jealousy and strife in his home is likened to one who has brought jealousy and strife upon the whole House of Israel,because everyone is a king in his own home..." (Esther 1:22).[14]

Furthermore, in the list of rabbis ordained by Rabbi Judah ben Bava[15] and that of the students of Rabbi Akiva,[16] it is Rabbi Meir who is mentioned first and not Rabban Simeon. When the latter became *Nasi*, he appointed Rabbi Natan, the son of the exilarch of Babylonia, as *Av Bet Din*, Rabbi Meir as Hakham (a newly created office in the Sanhedrin), and Rabbi Judah as the overseer (manager) of his household.[17] Thus, he indicated his desire for peace and harmony in the congress of the sages. Unfortunately, because of a tragic mistake, he did not succeed in achieving his aim.

In order to increase the prestige of the office of *Nasi*, Rabban Simeon changed a long-standing procedure in the Sanhedrin. When the *Nasi*, the *Av Bet Din* or the *Chacham* entered the hall, all present would rise and remain standing until the dignitary was seated. Rabban Simeon retained this custom with regards to himself, the *Nasi*, but changed it regarding the other two. For the *Av Bet Din* three rows were to rise as he passed them and then sit down; for the *Hakham* only one row at a time was to rise. Neither Rabbi Natan nor Rabbi Meir were present when this decision was taken and when they entered the hall on the following day they were disagreeably surprised. It is very likely that had they been consulted they would have agreed to the change but, as it was, they planned revenge. They decided that at the next session they would bring up problems in Tractate Uktzin, the last and one of the lesser-known tractates of the Talmud. They were sure that Rabban Simeon was not well versed in subject matter of this tractate and, when they had demonstrated his ignorance, they would put forward a motion to depose him; Rabbi Natan would then be *Nasi* and Rabbi Meir, *Av Bet Din*.

One of their colleagues, Rabbi Jacob, overheard them planning their coup and was concerned lest a scandal ensue and the *Nasi* be publicly shamed. So, sitting close to Rabban Simeon, he started loudly and demonstratively to study Uktzin. The latter realized that something was afoot so he too studied Uktzin intensively. When Rabbi Natan and Rabbi Meir sprang their trap, they were foiled because Rabban Simeon was able to handle all the problems they raised.

As a punishment for their impudence, he dismissed them from the study-hall. They continued sending questions into the court in writing. Those which Rabban Simeon could answer, he did ; and they themselves sent in the answers to the ones he could not. Finally, the sages in the academy came to the conclusion that this state of affairs could not be allowed to continue. How could these two great scholars be kept out of the study-hall?

Rabbi Simeon invited them back with the understanding that from now on neither of them should be mentioned by name. When a statement of theirs should have to be recorded in place of stating "Rabbi Meir said", one is to use the expression "others say", and in place of Rabbi Natan", the expression "some say" was to be used.[18]

Both Rabbi Natan and Rabbi Meir dreamt dreams telling them to return and apologise to Rabban Simeon. Rabbi Meir refused, saying that dreams could not affect his decision but Rabbi Natan returned to the study-hall and apologised to the *Nasi*. The latter accepted the apology with the extremely insulting remark, "The honor of your father, the exilarch of

Babylonia, helped you to become *Av Bet Din*; shall we therefore make you *Nasi* as well!?"[19]

This behavior seems hardly fitting for a man who devoted his whole self to the search for peace, yet, it is understandable. Rabban Simeon was defending the dignity of the office of *Nasi* and the honor of his illustrious family...., whereas he was prepared to forego his own dignity and allow a simple woman to spit on him, he could not forego the dignity of his office and genealogy and allow Rabbi Natan and Rabbi Meir to challenge his legitimacy. It is also possible that he believed that if Rabbi Natan were appointed *Nasi*, it would affect Eretz Israel's supremacy in Jewish life vis-a-vis the growing Jewish center in Babylonia. This thought may have motivated his remark to Rabbi Natan.

Rabban Simeon's manner of ruling the Sanhedrin led to the departure of several sages from that august body and new academies were started by them throughout the country: Rabbi Meir in Tiberias ; Rabbi Jose ben Halafta in Sepphoris; Rabbi Judah in Usha, his birthplace; Rabbi Eleazar ben Shammua in the Gallilee; and Rabbi Simeon in Tekoah.[20] These had all been disciples of and were ordained by Rabbi Judah ben Bava.[21] Assuredly they issued laws-rules and regulations which may not have conformed to the rulings of the Sanhedrin - under the presidency of Rabban Simeon. Rabban Simeon no doubt tried to counter-act this development by applyng the accepted ruling that "one *Bet Din* cannot abrogate the rulings of another, unless it is greater than it in both its size (i.e., number of judges) and its wisdom."[22]

These unhappy events had one very positive result: Torah academies were spread over the whole country and Torah study flourished. This growth is clearly indicated in the statement made by Rabbi Johanan: "When we studied with Rabbi Oshaiah, the study hall was so full that we sat four students to a cubit." Rabbi Judah the Nasi, Rabban Simeon's son, said, "When we studied with Rabbi Eleazar ben

Shammua, we sat six to the cubit."[23]

Our generation is privileged to witness the growth of Torah institutions both here in Israel as well as in the Diaspora, The study of Torah will, please G-d, bring truth and justice - and thus *peace*.

Notes

1. 4 Avot 1:18
2. *Semahot* 47a/b; *Avot D'Rabbi Natan* 32b/33a
3. *Avot* 1:2
4. *Gittin* 37b
5. *TJ Demai* 6:1
6. *Gittin* 45b
7. *TJ Berakhot* 7:1
8. *Kiddushin* 76a
9. *Bava Kama* 83a; *Sotah* 49b
10. *Midrash Rabbah, Genesis* 65:16
11. *Shabbat* 13b
12. *Gittin* 58a
13. *Nedarim* 66b
14. *Avot D'Rabbi* 28b
15. *Sanhedrin* 14a
16. *Yevamot* 62b
17. *Horayot* 13b
18. *Ibid*
19. *TJ Sotah* 1:4
20. *Sanhedrin* 32b
21. *Sanhedrin* 14a
22. *Avodah Zarah* 36a; *Gittin* 36b
23. *Eruvin* 53a

Rabbi Natan the Babylonian

Although the aim of this volume, A Companion to Avot, *is
to suggest events in the lives of the* tannaim *which might
have been the background to the moral dicta brought in their
names in Tractate Avot, chapters are included on Menahem
and Rabban Gamliel of Yavneh though none of their sayings
are incorporated in the tractate. Similarly, no* mishnah *in
the name of Rabbi Natan the Babylonian is to be found in
Avot, notwithstanding the fact that he was one of the
outstanding sages of his time. Indeed, Rabbi Natan served
as the* Av Bet Din *in the Sanhedrin under the presidency of
Rabban Simeon ben Gamliel and that of his son, Rabbi
Judah, the redactor of the Mishnah.*

Two possible reasons can be advanced for this strange
omission. The first is that Rabbi Natan compiled a volume very
similar in content to Avot. His work is known as *Avot D'Rabbi
Natan*, i.e., *The Avot of Rabbi Natan* or *Avot According to Rabbi
Natan*. It would appear that *Avot D'Rabbi Natan* is an earlier
compilation than our Tractate Avot because, Rabbi Judah the
Nasi was Rabbi Natan's junior and perhaps his pupil as is
evident from Rabbi Judah's statement of regret: "It was
childish of me to be presumptuous in the presence of Rabbi
Natan the Babylonian."[1] Furthermore, there is evidence that
Rabbi Natan assisted Rabbi Judah in the redaction of the
Mishnah.[2]

Tractate Avot follows the same order as *Avot D'Rabbi Natan*
except for Chapter 3 of the latter which does not appear in the
former. Another difference is the positioning of the *mishnayot*
of Rabban Johanan ben Zakkai. According to Avot, Rabban
Johanan ben Zakkai took over the leadership after Hillel and

Shammai,[3] but immediately after the latters' statements Rabbi Judah the Nasi brings aphorisms of his own ancestors starting with Rabban Gamliel I[4] and concludes Chapter One with the statement of his own father Rabban Simeon ben Gamliel.

He then begins Chapter Two with a *mishnah* of his own and one mishnah of his son,[5] Rabban Gamliel III, reverts to Hillel[6] and only then cites Rabban Johanan ben Zakkai.[7] In *Avot D'Rabbi Natan,*[8] however, Rabban Johanan is in his rightful position, i.e., immediately following Hillel and Shammai.[8]

Yet another difference between our Avot and *Avot D'Rabbi Natan* can be found in the general construction and character of the two works. *Avot D'Rabbi Natan* is replete with parables, informal statements and, the give and take of the sages in their discussions. Rabbi Judah condensed these statements and discussions and presents only the *mishnayot* in a terse, formal manner.

Some authorities view *Avot de Rabbi Natan* as a kind of *gemara* or commentary to Tractate Avot which does not have one of its own. Others consider it to be the *tosefta* to the Mishnaic tractate. Thus Rabbi Natan has a volume of his own, no need to offer a special Mishnah expressing his concept.

The second possible reason for the omission of Rabbi Natan from Avot may be the fact that he is never except in two places quoted by name in the Mishnah, but by the formula, "There are those who say...". Rabbi Natan had taken part, together with Rabbi Meir, in an unsuccessful attempt to depose Rabban Simeon ben Gamliel as *Nasi* of the Sanhedrin (See Chapter 13 for a full description of that incident). As a punishment, Rabban Simeon had ruled that the two should never be refered to by name, when their opinions were cited but that Rabbi Meir's traditions should be introduced with the formula, "Others say..." and Rabbi Natan's with, "There are those who say..."[9] Rabbi Judah the Nasi obviously had to follow his father's ruling. It could also be that he did not want to embarrass the memory of his teacher, Rabbi Natan, by quoting him with the required formula, "There are those who say." He preferred to leave him out altogether.

Once,[10] when Rabbi Judah taught his son, Simeon, a ruling which contained the formula, "Others say...," the latter asked, "Who are these 'Others' whose waters we drink (i.e., study their traditions) but whose names we do not mention?" Rabbi Judah explained that those were men "who tried to uproot your dignity and the dignity of your grandfather." "But," objected Simeon, "that happened a long time ago and the personalities are all dead and, anyway, they were not successful." Rabbi Judah replied, "That is correct, the enemies are no more, but the swords (the devastation) is forever" (Psalms 9:7). Rabbi Natan continued to serve as *Av Bet Din* even when Rabbi Judah succeeded his father as *Nasi*. He must have been a very old man when Rabbi Judah sent him and Rabbi Isaac on an important mission to Babylonia.[11]

During the Hadrianic persecutions, many sages had fled from Eretz Israel to other countries where they could practice Judaism openly and without fear. On the verse, "...but showing kindness to the thousandth generation of those who love Me and keep My commandments" (Exodus 20:6), the *Mekhilta*[12] quotes Rabbi Natan as saying that it refers to Jews who live in Eretz Israel and sacrifice their lives in order to observe the *mitzvot*. "Why are you being taken to be executed?" "Because I circumcised my son!" "Why are you being taken to be burned?" "Because I studied Torah!" "Why are you being crucified?" "Because I ate *matzah* on Pesah!"

Rabbi Natan's tragic interpretation of this verse is a clear reflection of the atrocities that were perpetrated against the Jewish population of Eretz Israel during Hadrian's reign and it is not difficult to understand - and indeed to sympathise with -, the many rabbis and scholars who fled the country in search of religious freedom.

According to the Talmud,[13] among the émigrés was Rabbi Hananiah, the nephew of the renowned Rabbi Joshua. He set up a *Bet Din* in Babylonia and began to regulate the calendar there. This involved fixing and proclaiming the New Moon (i.e., which day was *Rosh Hodesh*) and deciding on intercalation, i.e., in which years to add an extra month to bring the lunar cycle into line with the solar cycle (See Chapter 12) However, the leap year can only be proclaimed in Eretz Israel and if it is done anywhere else, the decision is null and void. Rabbi Judah the Nasi sent Rabbi Natan and Rabbi Isaac to Babylonia to prevail on Rabbi Hananiah to desist from the practice of intercalation. Rabbi Natan, being a Babylonian of noble descent, could be expected to wield great influence in the Jewish community there. At first, Rabbi Hananiah refused to accept the directive from Eretz Israel and went to consult Rabbi Judah ben Bathyra who advised him to accede to the demands of the Sanhedrin in Eretz Israel. When Rabbi Hananiah objected that his court was more qualified than that of Rabbi Judah the Nasi, Rabbi Judah ben Bathyra told him that the Almighty prefers a small group of scholars in Eretz Israel over the greatest Sanhedrin outside it.

It would appear that Rabbi Natan had had that thought in mind when he made *aliyah* to Eretz Israel. Being the son of the exilarch and a direct descendant of King David, there is no doubt that had he stayed in Babylonia, Rabi Natan would have succeeded to the exilarchy. The exilarch was the leader of the Jewish community and as such a man of great power who was the most respected and honored person in the Jewish community. Rabbi Natan was obviously of the opinion that it is preferable to be a lesser person in Eretz Israel than a leader outside it.

Rabbi Natan's love for Israel and especially for Jerusalem is best indicated by his statement[14] " ten measures of beauty was given to the world, Jerusalem possesses nine parts and the rest of the world one." His love for Torah is emphasized by his saying "ten measures of Torah descended to the earth. Nine portions are to be found in Israel and one in the rest of the world."

Just as Rabbi Natan had undertaken the mission to Babylonia in order to prevent a rift between the two largest Jewish communities in the world, so too he endeavored to make peace between individuals. He went so far as to state,[15] "it is a commandment" to offer a "white lie" in order to maintain harmony and argued, that even the Almighty Himself had demonstrated this. When the Almighty sent the prophet Samuel to annoint David as King of Israel, King Saul was still alive and would have killed Samuel had he known the truth. The Almighty, therefore, told the prophet that if Saul should ask him he should tell him that he was going to offer a sacrifice (Samuel I 16:2) although this was not true. Furthermore, when Sarah was informed that whe was to bear a child, she laughed in disbelief saying, "Now that I am old and withered, am I to have enjoyment - with my husband so old!?" But later we read: Then the Lord said to Abraham, 'why did Sarah laugh, saying, "shall I in truth bear a child, old as I am?" (Genesis 18:12-13). The Almighty did not tell Abraham that Sarah had also claimed that he, Abraham, was also too old to sire a child. All this to maintain family harmony!

Rabbi Natan's method of study was direct and logical. On the question as to the reason why it is permitted to desecrate the Sabbath in order to save a human life, the *Mekhilta*[16] cites answers given by many sages of which Rabbi Natan's is the most logical. He says that it is permitted to desecrate one Sabbath so that the person whose life is saved will be able to observe many Sabbaths. To explain why it is forbidden to offer wine to a Nazirite or a limb torn-off a living animal even to a non-Jew, Rabbi Natan[17] resorted to the verse: "You shall not place a stumbling block before the blind" (Leviticus 19:14), which he interprets to mean that it is forbidden to put temptation in anyone's path.

It seems that Rabbi Natan had some knowledge of medicine. Two incidents are recorded[18] regarding circumcision in which he offered medical advice which turned out to be correct. In both cases the first- and second-born sons had died as a result of circumcision and Rabbi Natan was asked whether the third-born sons should be circumcised. The accepted ruling is that a child whose two brothers died as a result of circumcision should not be circumcised since the two previous deaths indicate an hereditary medical problem in the family. Rabbi Natan, however, examined the children. One was very red and he suggested that the circumcision be delayed until the child's blood was better absorbed into his body. In the second case the child was greenish and Rabbi Natan advised the parents to wait with the circumcision until the child developed more blood. In both cases his advice was followed, the children were ultimately circumcised and no harm befell them. The grateful parents named both children, in honor of "Natan the Babylonian."

Rabbi Natan *is* mentioned by name, only twice in the Mishnah - probably, in Mishnayot uttered before the ruling, that no dictum of his shall be stated in his name. We do find the statement "It is said in the name of Rabbi Natan." Also in the Gemara and in the Beraitot we do find Rabbi Natan said-

It is therefore difficult to understand the Michilta that states "When Rabbi Natan died, his wisdom was lost with him." First because of the famous students that surely transmitted his thoughts, rulings-teachings - such as Rabbi Judah the Prince, Rabbi Matha b. Heresh and others. Most important, however, he left a very rich heritage in his famous Avot D'Rabbi Natan - Ethics According to *Rabbi Natan*.

Notes

1. *Bava Batra* 131a
2. *Bava Metzia* 86a
3. *Avot* 2:9
4. *Ibid*, 1:12-15
5. *Ibid*, 2:1-4
6. *Ibid*, 2:5-8
7. *Ibid*, 2-9
8. *Avot D'Rabbi Natan 14*
9. *Horayot* 13b
10. *Ibid*, 13b/14a
11. *TJ Sanhedrin* 1:2
12. *Mekhilta*, Yitro 20
13. *Berakhot* 63a; *TJ Sanhedrin* 1:2. In the Babylonian Talmud the two sages sent to Babylonia are identified as Rabbi Yose ben Kippas and the grandson of Zechariah ben Kebutal. In some sources the *Nasi* who initiated the mission is Rabban Simeon ben Gamliel.
14. *Midrash Rabbah*, *Esther* 1:7. A similar thought is to be found in the Talmud, Kiddushin 49b, albeit without mention of Rabbi Natan.
15. *Yevamot* 65b
16. *Mekhilta*, *Ki Tissa* 10:4
17. *Pesahim* 22b
18. *Hullin* 47b   *Shabbath* 134a
19. *Mekhilta*, *Yitro* 18

Rabbi Judah the Nasi

רַבִּי אוֹמֵר: אִיזוֹ הִיא דֶרֶךְ יְשָׁרָה שֶׁיָּבֹר לוֹ הָאָדָם, כָּל שֶׁהִיא
תִּפְאֶרֶת לְעֹשֶׂיהָ וְתִפְאֶרֶת לוֹ מִן הָאָדָם. וֶהֱוֵי זָהִיר בְּמִצְוָה קַלָּה
כְּבַחֲמוּרָה, שֶׁאֵין אַתָּה יוֹדֵעַ מַתַּן שְׂכָרָן שֶׁל מִצְוֹת,

> *Rabbi (Rabbi Judah the Nasi) said: Which is the right course
> that a man should choose for himself? One that does him
> honor and at the same time brings him honor from others. Be
> as careful with what seems to be a minor mitzvah as with one
> that seems to be important; for you do not know the reward
> given for the performance of a mitzvah...*[1]

Rabbi Judah, who lived in the 2nd and 3rd centuries
C.E., is also known in the Talmud by the simple appellation,
Rabbi[2] (perhaps because he is the rabbi *par excellence* in the
Jewish tradition), or *Rabbenu Hakadosh* (Our Holy
Teacher/Master).[3] It was Rabbi Judah who inaugurated the
redaction of the Mishnah, the basic formulation of the Oral
Law.

Clearly, the text of the Pentateuch must have been
accompanied by oral interpretations otherwise certain sections
would be unintelligible. The first to formulate and apply the
rules for interpreting the text of the Torah, was Moses himself
and indeed the authoritative law is always in accordance with
those rules laid down by Moses from Sinai.[4]

As the body of the Oral Law expanded in the course of the
generations through explanations and interpretations, some of
the Sages, such as Hillel the Elder, Rabbi Akiva and Rabbi

Meir, began to commit their traditions, decisions and reasoning to writing. It was becoming increasingly difficult to remember the oral interpretations of the Written Law both because of their enormous number and particularly since they were not studied in any sequence of subject matter or unifying theme. Perhaps Moses himself had foreseen this problem when he decreed that prior to a holiday only the laws of that holiday should be studied.[5]

Rabbi Judah the Nasi took upon himself the monumental task of collecting and collating all the decisions and explanations of the Oral Law and, adding his own opinions, classifiing all the material according to subject matter. He also rejected all those traditions (known as *Beraitot*) which were not authoritative enough to be taught in the major academies. Rabbi's work became the Mishnah, with its six "Orders": Seeds; Festivals; Women; Damages; Holy Things; and Purity. The Mishnah became the basis of the Talmud.

Avot, "The Ethics of the Fathers," which is one of the tractates in the Order of Damages, begins with a statement of the historical authenticity of the chain of transmission of the Oral Law: Moses received the Torah at Sinai and handed it on to Joshua who transmitted it to the elders[6]... Rabbi Judah goes on to list the transmission until his own times. He concludes Chapter 1 with his family lineage from Hillel the Elder till his own father, Rabbi Simeon ben Gamliel. Rabbi Judah himself was the seventh generation from Hillel who was a descendent of King David.[7]

Chapter 2 of Avot begins with Rabbi Judah's own aphorisms and, in a sense, one receives the impression of a comparison of Rabbi Judah to Moses. The latter handed down the Written Law and he, Rabbi Judah, the Oral Law. The Talmud seems to confirm this evaluation: Rabbah ben Rava said, "From Moses to Rabbi we do not find Torah and greatness in one place (i.e., one who was supreme in both Torah and worldly affairs)."[8]

Select a course that does you honor and brings you honor from others.

Rabbi Judah was a very wealthy man.[9] He made a wedding feast for his son, Simeon, on which he spent 24,000 *denari* (a large sum of money) but did not invite one of the outstanding scholars, Bar Kappara. This man, who was highly respected, felt insulted and did not try to hide his anger at the slight. Rabbi Judah realized that he had made a mistake and on a later occasion made it up to Bar Kappara. This incident could very well have been the classroom in which Rabbi learned which is the right course for a man to choose.

Once, during a serious famine, Rabbi Judah opened his store-houses to the needy but stipulated that only the learned could apply for help. One of his students, Rabbi Johanan ben Amram, disguised himself as a common peasant and demanded food because "God feeds even the animals and the birds" (Psalm 147:9). This powerful rebuke touched Rabbi Judah's conscience and he made his generosity available to everyone regardless of his scholarly attainments.[10] Might this not have been another lesson regarding which way a man should choose?

Be as careful with what seems to be a minor mitzvah as with one that seems to be important.

Rabbi Judah became ill "through an incident" and because of another incident was cured.[11] Once a calf on its way to the slaughterer broke away from its owner and ran to Rabbi, placing its head under his cloak as if to say "Save me!" Rabbi, however, returned it to its owner saying, "Go! For this you were created." In heaven they said, "Rabbi did not take pity on that calf, but just sent it away without trying to comfort it and thus ignored the law which forbids 'the pain of living creatures.'[12] Let us bring pain on him." Rabbi fell ill and suffered great pain.

How was he cured? One rainy, cold day the maid was cleaning the house and came across some newly born weasels lying in a corner. She wanted to sweep them out of the house but Rabbi told her: "Leave them. For it is written, 'And His tender mercies are over all His works' (Psalm 145:9)." In heaven they said, "Rabbi showed compassion for the young, let us show mercy on him!" And so he was cured and learned the value of a minor *mitzvah*.

> *You do not know the reward given for the performance of a mitzvah.*

It has been suggested that Rabbi Judah himself did know the specific value of each *mitzvah* and that this is the reason why he covered his eyes with his hand when he recited the first verse of the *Shema*[13] (a custom which has become universal). He wanted to block out of his mind the value of the *mitzvah* and concentrate only on accepting the yoke of the Kingdom of Heaven.

"And the sun rises and the sun sets" (Ecclesiastes 1:5); before the sun of one righteous man sets, the sun of another rises - on the day that Rabbi Akiva was martyred, Rabbi Judah was born.[14] For the Jews in Eretz Israel times were very hard. The Romans ruled with an iron hand. The practice of Judaism was proscribed by law. Jews were forbidden to study Torah, observe the Sabbath or circumcize their children. The penalty for transgressing these laws was death.

In order to show his disdain for such laws, Rabban Simeon ben Gamliel performed the circumcision of his son Judah, publicly, and he, his wife and the child were brought to trial. On their way to the court they stopped at the home of a Roman woman who had also just given birth to a son. This merciful woman begged Judah's mother to leave Judah with her and to take her son, Antoninus, who of course, was not circumcized, to the trial. When Rabbi Simeon ben Gamliel's case came before the judge, the uncircumcized child served as irrefutable evidence and the charge was dismissed. The amazed prosecutor exclaimed, "I personally witnessed the circumcision, but what can I do if their God performs miracles for them."[15]

Rabbi Judah and the gentile Antoninus remained steadfast friends for all their lives.

According to the Talmud,[16] this friendship was pre-ordained. When Rachel questioned the Almighty concerning her strange pregnancy, she was told, "Two nations (Hebrew: *goyim*) are in your womb" (Genesis 25:23) and it was taught in the name of Rav,"do not read *goyim* but rather *geyim*, outstanding men, and this refers to Rabbi and Antoninus (the first a descendant of Jacob and the other a descendent of Esau) from whose table radish, lettuce and cucumber were never absent in summer and in winter." What is the significance of this tradition?

It clearly indicates the friendship of these two great personalities, one the *Nasi* (President) of the Jews and the other, the Roman governor of Judea. It also indicates their great wealth which enabled them to serve summer vegetables even in winter. The rabbis of the Talmud may also be teaching us of the importance of vegetables in a balanced diet. However, I believe that the passage can be explained in an entirely different way.

Antoninus had an underground passage constructed from his palace to Rabbi Judah's home to enable them to visit each other without publicity.[17] This was particularly important in view of the significance of their respective positions. Now, when Antoninus visited Rabbi while he was dining, Antoninus could join him at the table. However, if Rabbi should visit Antoninus while he was eating, Rabbi could not join him because of the laws of *kashrut*. This could very well be the reason that the Talmud is at pains to inform us that each always had fresh uncooked vegetables on the table - Antoninus, so that Rabbi Judah could eat something and Rabbi Judah, so as not to embarrass Antoninus.

Many of the discussions Rabbi Judah and Antoninus held are revealed in the Talmud and the various *midrashim*. When Antoninus died, the Talmud uses the term "Passed away" which is usually reserved for the pious. At that time Rabbi Judah proclaimed: "The bond (of friendship) is snapped."[17] From this statement we can understand that Antoninus died before Rabbi. Antoninus ordered his son, who succeeded him, not to pass any laws against the Jews as long as Rabbi was alive,[18] and the Talmud states tersely: "When Rabbi died, troubles multiplied."[19]

From the above it is clear that the "troubles," i.e., the oppressive laws, were prepared during Rabbi's lifetime but were only put into effect when he died. This may explain two fascinating passages in the Talmud.[20]

When Rabbi was about to depart this life, he called for his sons. When they came he told them, "Be careful to show respect to your mother. Let the light (the candles) burn in its usual place, let the table be set in its usual place and let the bed be made up in its usual place."

Another of Rabbi's last wishes was with regards to his two sons and his pupil: "My son Simeon shall be the *Hakham* (i.e., the wise one, a position in the hierarchy of the Sanhedrin), my son Gamliel shall be the *Nasi* (i.e., his sucessor as president of the Sanhedrin); and Hanina ben Hama shall be the head of the academy." Was this the best last will and testament that Rabbi Judah could leave for his illustrious sons?

The Talmud devotes a great deal of discussion to the above passages. Rabbi's request to his sons, "show respect to your mother" raises an interesting question. Surely, they, the sons, were required by Biblical law to respect their mother. Why should Rabbi have stressed this? The explanation is that she was their step-mother and, according to law, children are only obliged to pay their step-mother the special respect due to a mother as long as their father is alive, as part of the respect due to him. Thus Rabbi was telling them that he wanted them to continue treating their step-mother as though he, Rabbi, was still alive. Perhaps this was out of appreciation for everything she had done for him and for them. This may also have been the reason for his request that the household be conducted as it was during his lifetime. We are told that every Friday evening Rabbi's soul visited his earthly abode to check that his last requests were being honored.

There is, however, another possible explanation. Rabbi Judah knew that as soon as he died, evil decrees would be enacted against the Jews. He therefore wanted to delay the publication of the news of his death as long as possible, so as to give the Jews that little extra period of peace. He therefore ordered his sons to behave as though he were still alive.

The law is that a mourner does not kindle all the lights but sits in semi-darkness; he does not eat at his usual place at table but by himself in a corner; he does not sleep in his usual bed but in one that has been "over-turned."[21] Rabbi, however, was willing to forego all the respect due to him as the *Nasi* as well as a father, and in effect was requesting his sons and colleagues to ignore his death for the good of the people. That is why the rabbis decreed that "Whoever says that Rabbi is dead, shall be pierced with a sword."

These passages, particularly the latter, present great difficulties. Were not all Jews required to mourn for a departed *Nasi* even as they had for Moses and Aaron? Indeed, Rabbi Hiyya[22] said that on the day Rabbi died "sanctity (of the *kohanim*, priests) is removed" since they too were required to attend the funeral of Rabbi whose remains were considered holy. Now we can readily understand why the rabbis threatened that, anybody who would publicize the *Nasi's* demise would be run through with a sword.

It is related[23] that the rabbis sent one of their colleagues, Bar Kappara, into the sick room to see how Rabbi Judah was faring. When he entered the room he saw that he was already dead and tore his cloak as a sign of mourning, as required by law. However, he rent the garment in a spot which would not be easily seen. When he returned to his colleagues they asked about the *Nasi's* condition and Bar Kappara answered: "The angels and the mortals struggled for the Ten Commandments and the angels won." "Do you mean that Rabbi is dead?" they asked. "You said it, not I," replied Bar Kappara.

Rabbi Judah the Nasi was an exceedingly complex personality. He was a true aristocrat. He was a descendant of one of the most illustrious families in Jewish history that of King David and, at the same time, was himself a man of outstanding erudition and ability. As such, he zealously guarded the honor of his position and his family; yet he was also capable of amazing humility. For him, the study of Torah and knowledge were the supreme values.

Rabbi Judah could not forgive Rabbi Meir for having demonstratively left the Sanhedrin during his father, Rabban Simeon ben Gamliel's, presidency and even went so far as to exclude Rabbi Meir's students from the academy after the latter's death, on the grounds, that they came to quibble and split hairs rather than study. When one of these students, Symmachus, forced his way in, Rabbi Judah exclaimed in rage, "Did I not say do not allow the students of Rabbi Meir to enter here ?"[24] Yet, Rabbi Judah based his Mishnah to a large part on Rabbi Meir's teaching albeit anonymously or with the preamble: "Others say..."[25] A possible explanation for Rabbi Judah's outbursts of anger is the fact that he suffered many years of illness and great pain and thus may have lost his temper.

Rabbi's deep understanding of human nature is reflected in his explanation of the discrepancy in the following Biblical verses.[26] In Exodus 21:12 we are told: "Honor your father and mother..." but in Leviticus 19:3 the command reads: "Every one should fear (revere) his mother and father." It is natural for a child to love - and therefore honor - his mother more than his father, because she soothes and persuades him with words during his rebellious moments. Therefore, the Bible, in the command to honor, puts the father first as if to say that you must also love and honor your father. Conversely, a person fears his father more than he does his mother for it is the father who instructs him in Torah. Therefore, in the command to fear, the mother is placed first to stress that she too must be feared and revered.

Rabbi Judah was also a kind and considerate person as is clear from some of his halakhic opinions. He tried to alleviate certain laws of tithes, fast-days and even holyday practices so as to make their observance easier on the people. He was also in an extremely delicate political position being in between his court, with its more extreme members, and the Roman administration in the Holy Land. Rabbi Judah even suggested[27] the curtailment of the fast of the 9th of Av, which commemorates the destruction of the two Temples, the second, at the hands of the Romans, when it falls on a Sabbath.

Above all, perhaps Rabbi Judah's humility in the presence of erudition was his outstanding characteristic. He was always prepared to admit that there were scholars who were greater than he[28] and on one occasion even went so far as to admit: "It was childish of me to be presumptuous in the presence of Rabbi Natan the Babylonian (a leading member of the Sanhedrin in Rabbi Judah's father's presidency).[29] On another occasion he revealed what is one of the greatest insights into the educational process: "Much have I learnt from my teachers; more, from my colleagues; but most, from my disciples!"[30]

As stated above, Rabbi Judah was very sensitive about his aristocratic genealogy but even in his pride he exhibited a rare measure of honesty. On one occasion he said: "If Rav Huna, the exilarch of the Babylonian Jewish community, were to come to Eretz Israel, I would give up my position in his favor; because he is from the Tribe of Judah being a descendant of King David through a son, while I am from the Tribe of Benjamin being descended from David only through a daughter."[28] Rav Huna did come to Eretz Israel but only after he had died - for burial.

The Talmud[32] relates that Rabbi Judah and Rabbi Hiyya were on a journey and came to a certain town. They asked the townsmen whether there was a scholar in their midst and were told that there was but he was blind. Rabbi Hiyya wanted Rabbi to stay at the inn while he, Hiyya, went to visit the blind scholar because he felt that it was beneath the dignity of the president of the Supremene Court, the Sanhedrin, to visit a rural scholar. Protocol demanded that the other scholar should visit Rabbi which he could not, being blind. For Rabbi, however, protocol did not exist when it came to honoring a scholar and he also went along. When he left the blind scholar's home he blessed them: "May you who have visited one who is seen but cannot see, be privileged to visit Him who sees but cannot be seen. Rabbi said: "Which is the correct course that a man should choose for himself? One that does him honor and at th : same time brings honor from others."

Notes

1. *Avot* 2:1
2. *Yevamot* 45a
3. *Shabbat* 118b
4. *Menahot* 29b
5. *Megillah* 4a
6. *Avot* 1:1
7. *Midrash Rabbah, Genesis* 98:13
8. *Gittin* 59a
9. *Nedarim* 50b
10. *Bava Batra* 8a
11. *Bava Metzia* 85a; *TJ Killaim* 9:3
12. *Shabbat* 128b

13. *Berakhot* 13b. I am indebted to Ha-Rav Ha-Gaon, Rabbi Abraham Kroll, for this insight.
14. *Kiddushin* 72b
15. *Avodah Zarah* 10b, *Tosafot*
16. *Avodah Zarah* 11a; *Berakhot* 57b
17. *Avodah Zarah* 10b
18. *Encyclopaedia Otzar Yisrael. Rabbi Judah the Nasi*
19. *Sotah* 49b
20. *Ketubbot* 103a
21. *Rambam, Mishneh Torah, Hilkhot Evel* 4:9, 5:18   *Yoreh Deah* 387a
22. *Ketubbot* 103b and see *Tosafot.*
23. *Ketubbot* 104a
24. *Kiddushin* 52b
25. *Sotah* 12a, *Tosafot*
26. *Kiddushin* 30b-31a
27. *Megillah* 5b
28. *Ketubbot* 103b; *Bava Metzia* 85b
29. *Bava Batra* 131a
30. *Makkot* 10a
31. *TJ Killaim* 9:3
32. *Hagigah* 5b

Rabban Johanan ben Zakkai

רַבָּן יוֹחָנָן בֶּן זַכַּאי קִבֵּל מֵהִלֵּל וּמִשַּׁמַּאי. הוּא הָיָה אוֹמֵר: אִם לָמַדְתָּ תּוֹרָה הַרְבֵּה אַל תַּחֲזִיק טוֹבָה לְעַצְמְךָ, כִּי לְכָךְ נוֹצָרְתָּ.

Rabban Johanan ben Zakkai received the tradition from Hillel and Shammai. He used to say: "If you have learnt much Torah, do not claim credit for it, because that is why you were created."[1]

Rabban Johanan ben Zakkai was the only sage who was not a descendant of Hillel to be honored with the appellation, *Rabban,* "Our teacher." He was deeply revered by his colleagues, by the general populace and even by the Roman authorities. We may assume that this is why he was given the title, although he had no right to it by reason of genealogy. Rabban Gamliel (II) of Yavneh was the rightful heir to the leadership being, as he was, a direct descendant of Hillel and an outstanding scholar, but at the time of the destruction of the Temple, he was either too young to assume the presidency of the Sanhedrin, or he was in hiding from the Romans who wanted to kill him and thus put an end to Hillel's progeny who were descendents from King David. The Romans viewed these dissidents as a threat to their hegemony over the area.

Rabban Johanan ben Zakkai's assumption of the leadership of the Sanhedrin constituted the fulfilment of a prophecy made by his teacher, Hillel the Elder.[2] Once, Hillel became ill and his students came to perform the *mitzvah* of *Bikkur Holim,* visiting the sick. All the students entered Hillel's room except Rabban Johanan who, out of humility, waited outside. Hillel asked,

"Where is the smallest of you (who makes himself small with regards to the rest of you; *Korban Ha-Edah*), who is a father to wisdom and a father to the generations and, needless to say, the greatest among you?" "He is in the courtyard," they answered. "Let him enter," Hillel requested. When Johanan ben Zakkai entered the room, Hillel recited a verse from the chapter on wisdom in the Book of Proverbs (8:21): "To cause those who love me to inherit substance and I will fill their treasure-houses." The term, "father to generations," is understood by the commentators to be a prophecy that Johanan ben Zakkai would become the *Nasi* of the Sanhedrin.

The introduction to our *mishnah*, "Rabban Johanan ben Zakkai received the tradition from Hillel and Shammai," is very significant. Rabban Gamliel (I), Hillel's grandson, had taught "Provide yourself with a teacher,"[3] which we have interpreted to mean that one authority should be appointed over all the sages of both Bet Hillel and Bet Shammai (see Chapter 10). The disagreements between the two outstanding academies had caused great doubt in the *Halakhah*, and Rabban Gamliel was advising that they be unified. Rabban Johanan ben Zakkai, having received his traditions from both the great masters, was accepted by the scholars of both schools. He thus, was able to unite them under his leadership.

It is indeed possible to understand Rabban Johanan's aphorism in our *mishnah* as an extension of a famous controversy that occupied Bet Hillel and Bet Shammai for two and one half years.[4] They had argued whether it was better for man to have been created or not. When the vote was taken, the school of Shammai's view prevailed: "It would have been better for man not to have been created; but now that he has, let him examine his deeds!" (See Chapter 7 for details of this discussion). The only way a man can "examine his deeds" is by studying Torah, because it is the Torah which establishes what good deeds are. Therefore, Rabban Johanan taught, if you have learnt much Torah, do not claim credit for it, for the study of Torah is the only justification for your having been created.

It is also possible to understand Rabban Johanan's dictum as an exhortation to his colleagues and a reflection on the times in which they lived. The Bible calls Torah *Tov* "Good," as is evident from the verse, "For I (the Almighty) have given you a *good* portion; do not desert My Torah" (Proverbs 4:2). The Hebrew for "do not claim credit for it" is *al tahzik tovah le-atzmekha* which can also mean, "do not keep the good to yourself." Thus, Rabbi Johanan is telling the other scholars: If you have studied a great deal of Torah, do not keep your knowledge to yourselves. Go out and teach it to others because that is why you were created. This was a particularly fitting exhortation in those times of crisis when only Torah could save the Jewish people. Rabban Johanan himself, set an example. The Talmud, in one passage,[5] relates that he used to sit in the shade of the Temple Wall all day long teaching Torah and, in another,[6] passage that he taught Torah for forty years.

The Talmud records that Hillel had eighty disciples.[7] He probably had many more but these eighty were worthy of special praise: thirty of them were so great that they deserved to have the Divine Presence rest upon them as it had on Moses; thirty were great enough to have miracles happen for them as for Joshua, for whom the sun stood still (Joshua 10:12-13), and the remaining twenty were average. The greatest of Hillel's disciples was Jonathan ben Uzziel, to whose scholarship even Shammai the Elder bowed,[8] and the smallest (*katan*) was Rabban Johanan ben Zakkai.

The question arises: If these scholars were indeed so great, then why did not the Divine Presence rest on thirty and why were miracles not performed for thirty? *Avot D'Rabbi Natan*[9] laconically explains that "their generation did not merit it."

In spite of the fact that Rabban Johanan was the smallest of the eighty, it was he who became *Nasi* of the Sanhedrin and the national leader. Surely the other seventy-nine disciples must have harbored some resentment at his appointment. One explanation is that the description "the smallest of them," is to be interpreted, according to the *Korban Ha-Edah* cited above, as "the one who makes himself the smallest," i.e., the humblest, and that the master, Hillel, had Prophesied that Rabban Johanan would be "the father of generations."

It is also possible that there was in fact some resentment on the part of the other disciples who considered themselves more learned than Rabbi Johanan, and that the aphorism in our *mishnah* is intended as a retort to them: If you know more Torah than I do, do not claim credit for it. The Almighty endowed you with better brains than He did me; do not praise yourselves - so were you created.

Yet another possible explanation for Rabban Johanan's advancement is that many of the eighty students - may have died during Hillel's long lifetime - after all, he lived to be 120 years - or they were killed by the Romans. The number of candidates for the presidency may have been reduced considerably and Rabban Johanan may have remained Hillel's most logical successor. Be the explanation to Rabban Johanan's appointment what it is , one thing is certain. The description, "the smallest," cannot refer to Rabban Johanan's age, because the Talmud[10] relates that he worked for forty years, studied Torah for forty years, and taught for forty years.

Rabban Johanan was adamant in his conviction that the study of Torah is the solution to all problems - personal and national. It is recorded[11] that there was a certain family in Jerusalem whose male children died at the age of eighteen. Distraught, the parents turned to Rabban Johanan. He told them: "You are, perhaps, the descendants of Eli the priest to whom the Almighty announced, '...all the increase of your house shall die in their youth' (I Samuel 2:33).Let them (your sons) study Torah and they will live." They did so and lived. The Talmud closes the incident by telling us that the children of that family were known as "Rabban Johanan's family."

Rabban Johanan was a most erudite scholar. The Talmud[12]

records that he had mastered the whole sea of Jewish learning. In addition, he exhibited many of the qualities of his saintly teacher, Hillel. Like Hillel, he too devoted himself to teaching;[13] he too was beloved by the masses and, we are told, always greeted everyone he met in the market-place, even non-Jews.[14] Hillel was a man of great humility as is dramatically illustrated in the stories of the would-be converts and the account of his encounter with the man who bet he could make Hillel lose his temper[15] (see Chapter 7). In this attribute of humility, Rabban Johanan also followed his teacher's example. We are told[16] that when his son became seriously ill, he went to his student, Rabbi Hanina ben Dosa, and asked him to pray for the child. Hanina prayed and the child recovered. Rabban Johanan remarked: "If I had prayed all day long, they (in Heaven) would have taken no notice" His wife objected: "Is then, Hanina greater than you?" "No," he answered. "But he is like a servant before the king (who goes into the king's presence at will), whereas I am like the king's minister (who only enters by invitation)."

Rabban Johanan ben Zakkai's piety and assiduity were proverbial. We learn[17] that profane talk never crossed his lips during his whole life, that he never walked four cubits without studying Torah and wearing *tefillin*, and that no one ever arrived at the study-hall before him or left it after him. No wonder then that he was chosen to lead the Jewish people.

It was Rabban Johanan's destiny to be one of the leading figures in the most dramatic event in Israel's history as a nation in its own land - the destruction of the Second Temple. Like his teacher, Hillel,[18] Rabban Johanan believed in peace and was in favor of making concessions to the Romans in order to stop the war. Jerusalem was under siege by the Roman legions. The population was starving and the various zealot factions were fighting for supremacy among themselves.

According to *Avot D'Rabbi Natan,*[14] Vespasian, the Roman commander, offered to lift the siege if the defenders would make a formal gesture of surrender, such as sending him a bow or an arrow, but the zealots refused. When Rabban Johanan heard of this "he sent for the men (leaders) of Jerusalem and said to them: My sons! Do you want to destroy the city and burn the Temple? What does he (Vespasian) want from you? All he wants is that you send him a bow or an arrow and he will leave.' They answered: 'Just as we killed his two predecessors, so will we go out against him and kill him.' Vespasian had spies in the city and they used to write everything they heard on paper, attach the notes to arrows and shoot them over the city walls. They informed Vespasian that Rabban Johanan ben Zakkai supported the emperor.

Rabban Johanan had foreseen the destruction of the Temple and Jerusalem.[20] During the forty years that preceded that terrible catastrophe there had been many portents. The miracles that had occurred in the Temple during Simeon the Tzaddik's tenure of office as High Priest, ceased during those years. The lot, "For the Lord," of the goats in the Yom Kippur Temple service always used to come up in the High Priest's right hand but now it appeared in accordance with the laws of chance. The Temple gates which were locked at night, were found open in the morning and Rabban Johanan rebuked them saying, "Sanctuary! Sanctuary! Why do you spread fear? I know that you will be destroyed and that Zechariah (Chapter 11:1) has already prophesied, 'Open, O Lebanon (i.e., the Temple), your doors and let fire consume your cedars.'"[21]

When he realized that there was no hope of persuading the zealots to make peace with the Romans, Rabban Johanan decided to escape from the city and try to save what he could. He let it be known that he was gravely ill and later his students announced that he had died. It is forbidden to leave a corpse in Jerusalem even overnight, thus two of his disciples, Rabbi Eliezer and Rabbi Joshua, carried him on a bier to the gates of the city, ostensibly to bury him outside the walls. The guard wanted to run the "corpse" through with his sword to make sure that it was dead but they objected: They (the non-Jews) will say, they (the Jews) even stabbed their rabbi! The guard then wanted to shake the body but Rabban Johanan's disciples made the same objection, so he allowed them to pass.[22]

When he arrived at the Roman camp, Rabban Johanan asked to see Vespasian, the commander of the Roman forces, and on entering his presence, hailed him as emperor. Vespasian replied: "You are deserving of death on two counts. Firstly I am not the emperor and secondly, if I were the emperor why did you not come earlier?" Raban Johanan answered him: "You will be emperor, for if you were not, Jerusalem would not fall into your hands since it is written, 'The Lebanon (i.e., the Temple) will fall to a great one' (Isaiah 10:34) and 'a great one' means a king; and as far as my not coming earlier is concerned, the zealots among us would not allow me."

They had hardly finished this conversation when a messenger arrived from Rome and informed Vespasian that the Emperor had died and that the Senate had elected him to that position. As the messenger spoke Vespasian was putting on his boots. He had already laced one boot, but, upon hearing the news, he was unable to get the other boot on. Rabban Johanan told him to bring someone he hated into his presence. He did so, and then his foot slipped into the second boot. Rabban Johanan explained this phenomenon by citing two verses from the Book of Proverbs: "...a good report makes bones fat" (15:30) while "...a broken spirit (i.e., displeasure) dries out the bones"(17:22).[22]

Vespasian was so impressed with Rabban Johanan that he granted his requests: to grant him the city of Yavneh and its sages; to spare the family of Rabban Gamliel (which the Romans would presumably have killed in order to wipe out Israel's leadership); and a cure for Rabbi Zadok who had fasted for forty years trying to stave off the destruction of the Temple.

It is interesting to note that Josephus[23] tells a similar story but with himself as the hero who prophesied Vespasian's election as emperor. Josephus had been the commander of the Jewish forces in the Galilee and had out-maneuvered the Jewish leadership in Jerusalem in all its attempts to remove him from the position. Finally, taking cover in a cave while escaping from the Romans, he convinced the men with him to commit suicide rather then fall into Roman hands. He survived and went over to the enemy. As an important figure in the Jewish revolt, he was welcomed and he ingratiated himself with Vespasian by informing him that he was elected emperor. He was accepted into the Roman's family and even adopted the family name, Flavius. In his entire account of the revolt, Josephus does not mention Rabban Johanan ben Zakkai even once, although he does mention several of the other leading sages of his time.

The fact that Rabban Johanan asked Vespasian for Yavneh *and its sages* indicates that during this period there already was an established academy there. Rabban Johanan wanted to move the center of religious life in Eretz Israel from Jerusalem, which he knew would be destroyed, to the quiet town of Yavneh. Since he had received Vespasian's agreement, Yavneh would henceforth be under his protection and many sages would come there because there they would be immune from persecution. Ultimately, according to the Talmud,[24] Rabbi Zadok was cured and Rabban Gamliel came out of hiding and assumed his rightful position as *Nasi* of the Sanhedrin which was now in Yavneh. Rabban Johanan became *Av Bet Din.* The Talmud[25] also reports that some sages, notably Rabbi Akiva, criticized Rabban Johanan for not taking advantage of his moment of grace with Vespasian by asking him to lift the siege altogether. Rabban Johanan felt that that would have been too risky; if Vespasian had refused, they would not have had even a "small salvation."

Rabban Johanan was now faced with the reconstruction of Jewish life and like his teacher, Hillel, he was not afraid to inaugurate several important *takkanot*, new laws, to meet the critical situation. He ruled[26] that when Rosh Ha-Shanah falls on a Sabbath, the *shofar* should be sounded as it had been in the Temple but only in those places where there was an official *Bet Din*. On this ruling he stood firm against the objections of the Benei Bathyra. He also ruled[27] that on Sukkot, the *arba'ah minim* (the *lulav* and *etrog* etc.) should be taken and waived all seven days of the festival, again as they had done in the Temple. The aim of these *takkanot* was two-fold: Firstly, he wanted to keep the Temple procedures alive in the hearts of the people in the hope that it would spedily be rebuilt and, secondly, he wanted to establish the authority of the Sanhedrin which would be so necessary to steer the Jewish people through the turbulent times ahead.

In addition to his abilities as a scholar and a national leader, Rabban Johanan was also blessed with the talent to create parables which is so important in conveying abstract philosophical and theological ideas to ordinary people. In the Talmud we learn[28] that Rabbi Eliezer taught that a person should repent one day before he dies. His students asked: "Does anyone know when he is going to die?" to which Rabbi Eliezer answered, "That is exactly the point! He must repent today lest he die tomorrow thus a person should be repenting all his days." And so too Solomon said in his wisdom, at all times, let your garments be white...' (Ecclesiastes 9:8).

This is a profound idea which not everybody is capable of understanding. Rabban Johanan clothed it in a beautiful parable to make it understandable to all: This may be compared to a king who summoned his servants to a banquet without fixing the precise time. The wise among them prepared themselves immediately and sat waiting at the gate of the palace, for they reasoned, 'Is anything lacking in the royal palace? The king may call us at any moment.' The fools went about their ordinary work, reasoning, 'Can a banquet he held without preparation? We have time.' Suddenly the king announced the banquet. The wise servants entered and took their appointed places at the tables but the fools had to stand in their soiled working-clothes and look on with envy." The King, of course, is the Almighty; the banquet is the World-to-Come; the wise servants are those who have prepared themselves and are ready. This parable sacrifices nothing of Rabbi Eliezer's profundity in making the idea sparklingly clear to even the most simple mind.

The Talmud[29] gives an account of Rabban Johanan ben Zakkai's death which is extremely touching and instructive:

When Rabban Johanan ben Zakkai became ill, his disciples came to visit him. When he saw them he began to weep. They said to him: "Light of Israel! Right-hand column! Mighty hammer! Why do you weep?" He answered: "If they were taking me before a king of flesh and blood, who is here today but in the grave tomorrow, whose anger is not everlasting and if he imprisons me it is not for ever and if he executes me it is not eternal death, whom I can appease with words and bribe with money, would I not weep? Now, they are bringing me before the supreme King of Kings, who exists forever, whose anger is everlasting; if He imprisons me it will be forever and if He executes me it will be eternal death, whom I cannot appease with words or bribe with money. Furthermore, there are two ways open before me, Paradise and Hell, and I do not know to which they are taking me, should I not weep?

"Our teacher," they said, "bless us!"

"May the fear of heaven be as strong on you as the fear of man!"

"Is that all?" they wondered.

"Would that it were so," he said. "Know you, when a man commits a crime, he thinks 'can anyone see me?'" As he was dying he said to them: "Take all the utensils out of the house and prepare a chair for Hezekiah, king of Judah, who is coming."

Rabban Johanan's last words demand some explanation

and indeed they are extraordinarily significant. Rabban Johanan believed with all his heart that the Temple would be rebuilt and that the laws of ritual purity and impurity would once again become very practical laws. This is the meaning of his demand to take all the untensils out of the house so that they should not become ritually impure from the impurity attached to a corpse.

Similarly, his reference to King Hezekiah is generally understood as an expression of his faith in the restoration of Israel's sovereignty. But if that is so, why Hezekiah? Why not King David? However, it is possible to interpret the reference as being to himself, and the most important decision he ever made. At that moment, the last of his life, Rabban Johanan was stricken with doubt. When he had stood before Vespasian, he had believed that no place, not even Jerusalem with its Temple and sanctity, can save Israel; only the knowledge and the observance of Torah can do that. That belief had led him to ask for Yavneh and its sages, because this would ensure the continuation of Torah study. Now, as he had contemplated coming before the supreme King of Kings, he was not so confident that he had made the right decision then. Perhaps he should have asked for Jerusalem and the Temple notwithstanding the risk involved. He was then granted a vision. During his moment of dilemma, he saw King Hezekiah whose outstanding achievement had been the propagation of Torah knowledge throughout the land. Hezekiah had so concentrated on this that in his times, we are told, "there was not a boy or a girl, a man or a woman, from Dan to Beersheba, who was not entirely conversant with the complicated laws of purity and impurity."[30] King Hezekiah's system had been successful. For when the Syrian, Sennacherib, had besieged Jerusalem, the city had been miraculously saved; the Syrians had all perished in one night. Thus, this revelation constituted a heavenly assurance to him that he had made the right decision.

The Sages said[31] that when Rabban Johanan died, "the glory of wisdom ceased." A prophecy made by his teacher Hillel the Elder declared that Rabban Johanan, "the smallest" of his students, would be "the father of generations." And that prophecy was surely fulfilled. Rabban Johanan ben Zakkai saved Judaism in its most critical hour and thus became the father of all subsequent generations of Jews.

Notes

1. *Avot* 2:9
2. *TJ Nedarim* 5:6
3. *Avot* 1:16
4. *Eruvin* 13b
5. *Pesahim* 26a
6. *Rosh Ha-Shanah* 31b
7. *Bava Batra* 134a
8. *Ibid*
9. *Avot de Rabbi Natan* 14:1
10. *Rosh Ha-Shanah* 31b
11. *Rosh Ha-Shanah* 18a; *Yevamot* 105a
12. *Bava Batra* 134a
13. *Pesahim* 66a - 26a
14. *Berakhot* 17a
15. *Shabbat* 31a
16. *Berakhot* 34b
17. *Sukkah* 28a
18. *Avot* 1:12
19. *Avot D'Rabbi Natan* 4:5 - 20b
20. *Yoma* 39b
21. *Ibid*
22. *Gittin* 56a; *Avot D'Rabbi Natan* 4:5 - 20a
23. *Josephus, Wars* 3:8-9
24. *Gittin* 56b
25. *Ibid*
26. *Rosh Ha-Shanah* 4:1
27. *Ibid*
28. *Shabbat*
29. *Berakhot* 28b
30. *Sanhedrin* 94b
31. *Sotah* 49a

Rabbi Eliezer ben Hyrcanus

רַבִּי אֱלִיעֶזֶר אוֹמֵר: יְהִי כְבוֹד חֲבֵרְךָ חָבִיב עָלֶיךָ כְּשֶׁלָּךְ, וְאַל תְּהִי
נוֹחַ לִכְעֹס, וְשׁוּב יוֹם אֶחָד לִפְנֵי מִיתָתְךָ, וֶהֱוֵי מִתְחַמֵּם כְּנֶגֶד
אוּרָן שֶׁל חֲכָמִים, וֶהֱוֵי זָהִיר בְּגַחַלְתָּן שֶׁלֹּא תִכָּוֶה, שֶׁנְּשִׁיכָתָן
נְשִׁיכַת שׁוּעָל, וַעֲקִיצָתָן עֲקִיצַת עַקְרָב, וּלְחִישָׁתָן לְחִישַׁת שָׂרָף,
וְכָל דִּבְרֵיהֶם כְּגַחֲלֵי אֵשׁ.

*Rabbi Eliezer ben Hyrcanus said: Let the honor of your
fellow be as dear to you as your own. Be not easily provoked
to anger and repent one day before you die. Warm yourself
by the fire of the scholars but beware of their glowing coals
lest you be burned; for their bite is the bite of the fox and
their sting is the sting of the scorpion and their hiss is the hiss
of the serpent and all their words are like coals of fire.*[1]

Rabbi Eliezer was the son of a successful landowner and, in his
youth, worked on his father's holdings. He had not studied
more than was usual for one of his class and could be described
as as *am ha-aretz*, an ignoramus as far as Torah study was
concerned.[2] According to one source[3] he did not even know
how to recite the *Shema*.

We do not know what caused his change of heart but one
day, when he was twenty-two years old, he told his father that
he wanted to go to Jerusalem to study Torah with Rabban
Johanan ben Zakkai. According to another source,[3] he was
twenty-eight years of age and, after fasting for two weeks,
Elijah the Prophet appeared to him and told him to go to
Jerusalem to study with Rabban Johanan.

Hyrcanus, his father, became angry and said, "You will not

get anything to eat until you plough a full field!" Eliezer rose early the following morning and ploughed the field. That day was a Friday and instead of going to his parents' house he went to his parents-in-law to eat. Another version[3] claimed that he fasted from midday on Friday until midday on Sunday. When he was walking on his way to Jerusalem he spotted a stone which looked like food and he was so hungry that he put it in his mouth. Some say that it was a stone but others say that it was a piece of cattle dung.

In Jerusalem he found a place to lodge and sat at Rabban Johanan ben Zakkai's feet and studied Torah until the latter became aware of his bad breath which was caused by hunger since he had no money to buy food but was too proud to say so. Rabban Johanan asked him whether he had eaten but Eliezer did not reply. Rabban Johanan called the owner of the house where Eliezer was lodging and asked him if he had eaten there. "No," he answered, "I thought he was eating with you." "And I," said Rabban Johanan, "thought he was eating with you. Between us we nearly lost Rabbi Eliezer."

Soon Rabbi Eliezer became one of Rabban Johannan's outstanding disciples. When the latter described the abilities of his five best students,[4] he compared Rabbi Eliezer to "a cemented cistern which does not lose a drop," i.e., he never forgot a word of what he had learned, and commented further[5] that "if all the sages of Israel were put in one balance of a scale and Rabbi Eliezer ben Hyrcanus in the other, he would outweigh them all." Heady praise indeed. The Talmud[6] recounts that when the sages, and Rabbi Eliezer among them, were gathered in Yavneh a voice from heaven declared: "There are two among you, Samuel Ha-Katan and Rabbi Eliezer, who are worthy that the Divine Spirit should rest on them but the generation is not worthy of such an honor."

Rabbi Eliezer was totally devoted to his teacher, Rabban Johanan ben Zakai, and he refused to give decisions of questions of law unless he had heard them from his teacher. Even when he did answer he did so by quoting Rabban Johanan *verbatim*. We are told[7] that once when Rabbi Eliezer was visiting the Upper Galilee he was asked 30 questions concerning the laws of the *sukkah*. He answered 18 of them but refused to answer the other 12 on the grounds that "I have not heard these questions answered by my teacher."

Thus did Rabbi Eliezer rise from obscurity to become one of Rabban Johanan's most faithful and trusted disciples and indeed he and his colleague Rabbi Joshua were the ones who assisted Rabban Johanan to escape from besieged Jerusalem to meet the Roman commander, Vespasian, and save Judaism.[8]

The Mishnah[9] records that the venerable Rabban Johanan asked his five outstanding pupils to give their opinions as to "the good way to which a man should cleave." Rabbi Eliezer's contribution to the discussion was "a good eye," i.e., the virtue of looking kindly on everyone and everything. When the pupils were asked to describe "the evil way that a man should shun" Rabbi Eliezer answered, "an evil eye," i.e., the vice of seeing only the bad in people.

Each of the five disciples also offered three pieces of ethical advice.[10] The first of Rabbi Eliezer's was, "Let the honor of your fellow be as dear to you as your own," which thought is also expressed in the Talmud[11] in the following form: When Rabbi Eliezer became ill his students came to visit him. They said to him "Our teacher, instruct us in the way of life so that through them we may merit the life-to-come." He said to them, "Be heedful of the honor of your colleagues..."

Clearly, the consideration a person must show for his fellow's honor was an important ingredient in Rabbi Eliezer's ethical-philosopical system and the question that arises is: Why did Rabbi Eliezer place so much emphasis on this point?

The Talmud[12] tells of an event in which Rabbi Eliezer was the central figure, and which had tragic consequences which might explain his preoccupation with the respect every man owes his fellow man. A discussion began among the sages with regard to a special type of oven constructed of small ceramic tiles with a layer of sand between them. Rabbi Eliezer argued that since each individual tile was too small to be considered a "vessel" (or "utensil") and since there was sand between the tiles, the whole oven could not become ritually impure. The other rabbis, however, claimed that the whole oven was an earthenware vessel and as such did become ritually impure when exposed to the conditions that cause such impurity, and, would then have to be broken up. Rabbi Eliezer was in a minority of one, but adamantly refused to accept the majority decision which is the accepted procedure.

To make his point he declared, "If I am right, may that carob tree prove it." The carob tree moved one hundred cubits. In the account of the event in the Jerusalem Talmud,[13] one of the commentators, Korban Ha-Edah, claims that at Rabbi Eliezer's command, the carob tree also returned to its original place. But the rabbis said, "You cannot bring proof from a carob tree!" Rabbi Eliezer insisted and said, "If I am right, may the water in this aqueduct flow backwards!" It did - but the rabbis said, "You cannot bring proof from the water in an aqueduct." "May the walls of the study-hall prove that my view is correct." and the walls began to incline and keel over. Rabbi Joshua rebuked the walls harshly: "If the scholars are discussing a point of law, what business is it of yours?" To maintain the honor of Rabbi Joshua the walls did not fall but, for the sake of Rabbi Eliezer's honor, they did not straighten out.

Rabbi Eliezer, however, would not yield and declared, "If I am right, may the very heavens prove it!" and a voice came from heaven and said, "Why are you distressing Rabbi Eliezer? The law is according to his opinion in everything." At this Rabbi Joshua arose and declared: "It (the Torah) is not in heaven," an allusion to Deuteronomy 30:12. The Talmud proceeds to explain this as meaning that since the Torah itself rules "You must follow the majority," Exodus 23:2 according to the accepted rabbinic interpretation) the law does not go according to voices from heaven.

Rabbi Eliezer still refused to accept the majority decision and a vote was taken in the accademy and he was excommunicated. Rabbi Akiva volunteered to go and inform Rabbi Eliezer of the Sanhedrin's verdict. Rabbi Akiva was afraid that if a less tactful person did so, Rabbi Eliezer might become so upset and angry that his furious glare would destroy all about him. Rabbi Akiva dressed in black, went to Rabi Eliezer's home and sat down in front of him at a distance of four cubits, it being forbidden to come closer than that to a person who is under a ban. "Why," asked Rabbi Eliezer, "is this day different from other days?" "My teacher," answered Rabbi Akiva, "it seems to me that the rabbis are staying away from you." At this Rabbi Eliezer rent his garments, removed his shoes, sat on the ground and wept - as if he was mourning for himself.

On that day one third of the olives, wheat and barley in the world were destroyed and some say that even the dough being kneaded by women went sour. Rabban Gamaliel, the *Nasi*, was on board ship on the day that Rabbi Eliezer, who was his brother-in-law, having married his sister, was told of the ban and a huge wave threatened to engulf the ship. Rabban Gamaliel understood that "this must be because of Rabbi Eliezer ben Hyrcanus" and he stood and made the following declaration to heaven: "Lord of the universe! You know that I did not do it for my own honor or for the honor of my father's house but only for Your honor so that divisions (on halachic matters) should not increase in Israel!" The sea became calm.

The story of Rabbi Eliezer's excommunication raises a most perplexing question. Surely he knew that the law must follow the majority. Why then did he refuse to accept its decission in this case? In order to understand Rabbi Eliezer's position in this matter, it would be helpful to review some of the circumstances surrounding his career and status in the rabbinic world of the time. He was known as Rabbi Eliezer the Elder which is a most important and prestigious appellation and Onkelos' famous translation of the Torah was made under his guidance[14]. He never forgot even an iota of what he had learned[4] and never handed down a decision unless he had heard it from his teachers.[7]   Furthermore, his own teacher, the great Rabban Johanan, had described him as being more worthy than all the other sages put together and in that generation nearly all the sages had also been students of Rabban Johanan. It may therefore be that Rabbi Eliezer did not see the dispute over the oven as a matter of the individual versus the majority but rather as a dispute between the students of Rabban Johanan and that he was the best equipped to say what the master would have ruled. He believed that his decisions should be accepted by virtue of his status - but they were not, and he was excommunicated.[12]

Is it any wonder, then, that Rabbi Eliezer counseled his own disciples, "Let the honor of your fellow be as dear to you as your own?" He felt that his honor had been besmirched and that he had not been treated justly. His own brother-in-law, Rabban Gamaliel, his closest colleague, Rabbi Joshua, and his dear student-colleague, Rabbi Akiva, had allowed the Sanhedrin to place him under a ban.

Rabbi Eliezer's behavior in another matter also presents a difficulty. Although he had been an ignoramus when he had presented himself before Rabban Johanan and asked to be accepted as a student, the latter had not placed any obstacles in his way but had accepted him readily and with great warmth and had given him the attention and the encouragement that made it possible for him to become one of his five outstanding pupils. Yet, when Akiva, the ignorant forty-year old shepherd came before Rabbi Joshua and Rabbi Eliezer and begged to be taught, Rabbi Eliezer coldly ignored him.[15] It took Rabbi Akiva thirteen years until he rendered an opinion in a Torah discussion and then, Rabbi Joshua who had always recognized his tremendous potential, quoted to Rabbi Eliezer a verse, "Is this not the people you rejected? Go out now and do battle with him!" (Judges 9:38), as much as to say, "Rabbi Eliezer, you have met your match!"

Now, Rabbi Eliezer followed Rabban Johanan's philosophy and way of life faithfully; why did he not accept Rabbi Akiva as a student with the same grace that Rabban Johanan had accepted him? It is possible that Rabbi Eliezer believed that, at forty years of age, Akiva was too old to study. Furthermore, before he had worked as a shepherd for Kalba Savua, Rabbi Akiva had worked as a farm-hand on Rabbi Eliezer's estate. Rabbi Eliezer just could not see this ignorant lowly workman developing into a real scholar. His own case had been different. Although he had been an ignoramus, he nevertheless was a member of a wealthy, aristocratic, landed family. However, after the initial, long-lasting coldness, we find many instances[16] of Rabbi Akiva's name being coupled with those of Rabbi Eliezer and Rabbi Joshua. Rabbi Akiva himself showed great respect, fondness and understanding towards Rabbi Eliezer, as we shall see.

Rabbi Eliezer ben Hyrcanus was not an easy person to get along with, especially when his views were not accepted or his requests ignored. On one occasion[17] he ordained a series of thirteen fast days because of drought. On the last of them, when rain had still not fallen, the assembled people began to leave the synagogue. Rabbi Eliezer scolded them saying, "Have you prepared graves for yourselves?" The people began to groan and weep and it began to rain.

On another occasion,[18] Rabbi Eliezer stood before the Holy Ark and offered twenty-four benedictions asking for rain but the drought continued. Rabbi Akiva then went and stood before the Ark and pronounced three benedictions and it began to rain. A voice from heaven declared that the rain had come not because Rabbi Akiva was a greater scholar than Rabbi Eliezer but because he was an easy-going forgiving person, which Rabbi Eliezer was not.

From these incidents it is clear that once Rabbi Eliezer made up his mind on a subject, law or person, he found it difficult to change his attitude. This may be the reason why he had so much difficulty in accepting Rabbi Akiva as a student — he still saw him as an ignorant farm-hand. Later in life, however, he mellowed and advised his students, "Be not easily provoked to anger..."[19]

Although the *mishna*[20] states,"They (the five disciples of Rabban Johanan) each said three things," more than three are given in the name of Rabbi Eliezer. His *mishnah* continues with, "Warm yourself by the fire of the scholars but beware of their glowing coals lest you be burned." How well this reflects Rabbi Eliezer's own character. We have seen how much damage was caused by his anger. It is as though he was drawing a lesson from his own experience — sit at the feet of the sages but take care not to provoke them to anger. The dictum may also reflect another aspect of his own career — he had warmed himself by the fire of the sages but had come too close and had been burned.

Apparently the ban pronounced on Rabbi Eliezer was not strictly adhered to by the other scholars. It seems that all it meant was that he was not permitted to attend meetings at the academy and that the other sages could not consult with him on matters of law. We do find, however, that students continued to study in his *yeshiva* in the town of Lod.[21] Rabbi Joshua, who had been the main protagonist in the dispute about the oven, once kissed the stone on which Rabbi Eliezer used to sit while lecturing saying, "This stone can be compared to Mount Sinai and the one who sits on it to the Ark of the Covenant."[23]

When Rabbi Eliezer became ill[24] his students visited him and he told them, "There is a fierce wrath abroad in the world." Rashi explains that he was referring to himself since the Almighty must be angry with him to inflict such great pain on him. Hearing this the students wept but Rabbi Akiva laughed. "Why do you laugh?" they asked. "Why do you weep?"

countered Rabbi Akiva. "A Torah Scroll is in such agony, should we not weep!" " That is precisely why I laugh," said Rabbi Akiva. "Until now I saw that Rabbi Eliezer prospered in all his financial endeavors and I was afraid lest the Almighty was rewarding him in this world for all the good he has done. Now, however, when I see him suffering great pain, I am certain that he will receive and enjoy his proper reward in the world-to-come." Rabbi Eliezer then asked Rabbi Akiva, "Have I neglected anything of the whole Torah?" to which Rabbi Akiva, in his sublime tact, answered, "Master, did you not yourself teach us 'There is no man righteous on earth who has done only good and not sinned' (Ecclesiasties 7:20)?"

On the same folio of the Talmud we are told of another visit to the dying Rabbi Eliezer — this time by the four great sages, Rabbis Tarfon, Joshua, Eleazar ben Azariah and Akiva. Rabbi Tarfon comforted him with, "You are more valuable to Israel than the rain; because the rain is only good for this world while you are good for Israel in this world and the world -to-come." Rabbi Joshua told him that he was more precious to Israel than the sun for the same reason and Rabbi Eleazar ben Azariah said that he was more valuable than parents because parents only bring their child into this world while Rabbi Eliezer ben Hyrcanus directs his students in the world and helps them to merit the World-to-Come.

Rabbi Akiva, however, merely remarked, "Suffering is to be welcomed!" At this, Rabbi Eliezer asked them to sit him up so that he could "hear his pupil, Akiva" and asked, "Akiva, where so you know that from?" "From the Bible," answered Akiva. "King Menasseh was exceedingly wicked and all the efforts of his pious father, King Hezekiah, did not succeed in reforming him. Yet when he suffered physical pain at the hands of the Assyrians he turned to God and was forgiven and even restored to his throne in Jerusalem. Thus you see that suffering is to be welcomed!" Once again Rabbi Akiva exhibited his enormous understanding of human beings and his great sympathy with them. He knew that Rabbi Eliezer was totally preoccupied with his fate in the World-to-Come particularly in view of the fact that he had been excommunicated and, as in the previously cited visit, found a way to interpret Rabbi Eliezer's suffering in order to comfort and console him.

On another page of the Talmud[24] we read that when Rabbi Eliezer was ill and Rabbi Akiva and his companions visited him, he was sitting up in his canopied bed as it was late on Friday afternoon. The visitors sat and waited outside in the hall. Rabbi Eliezer's son, Hyrcanus, approached his father to remove his *tefillin*, which are not worn at night or on Sabbaths and Holydays, but Rabbi Eliezer rebuked him and he went away shamefacedly. "It seems to me," that my father's mind is deranged," he said to the waiting rabbis. Rabbi Akiva, however,[25] countered, "Rabbi Eliezer is in order, but Hyrcanus and his mother aren't. Here it is nearly Shabbat and the candles are not yet kindled nor has the food been put into the oven to keep it warm for the Sabbath. To do these things on Shabbat is a transgression of Biblical law as it is written, 'You shall kindle no fire...on the Sabbath day' (Exodus 35:3), whereas wearing *tefillin* on Shabbat is only a Rabbinic prohibition."

Realizing that Rabbi Eliezer was lucid, the visiting rabbis went into his room and sat before him at a distance of four cubits. "Why have you come?" demanded Rabbi Eliezer of them. "To study Torah," they answered. "But where have you been until now?" "We had no time." "I will be surprised," said Rabbi Eliezer, "if you will die natural deaths." At this, Rabbi Akiva asked, "and mine?" "Yours," answered Rabbi Eliezer, "will be the worst of all because, with your capacity, had you come to study with me you would have learnt a great deal of Torah."

Rabbi Eliezer then lifted his arms, folded them across his chest and cried, "Woe to you, my two arms for you are like two rolled Torah Scrolls (in which the text is covered, so too his learning had been concealed because the sages did not come to consult with him - Rashi). Much have I learned and much have I taught. Much have I learned - yet I did not take from my teachers even as much as a dog lapping from the sea. Much have I taught - yet my pupils have taken from me only as much as a paint-brush takes from its tube... I studied three hundred - some say, three thousand - laws about planting cucumbers yet nobody, except Rabbi Akiva, ever asked me a question on the subject..."

On that occasion, the rabbis asked him many questions on matters of ritual impurity and he answered each one, proclaiming the impure to be impure and the clean to be clean. He died as he pronounced the word, "Clean!" and Rabbi Joshua stood up and proclaimed, "The ban is lifted! The ban is lifted!"

In the version of this incident as it is recorded in *Avot D'Rabbi Natan*[26] an additional insight is given. After Rabbi Eliezer gave his decisions to the rabbis about what was ritually pure and what was impure, he said, "I fear that the disciples of this generation will be punished by death from heaven (i.e., an unnatural death)." "Why?" "Because they did not attend on me." Then Rabbi Eliezer turned to Rabbi Akiva and asked him, "Akiva! Why did you not come and attend on me?" "I had no time." "I doubt whether you will die a natural death." At this point Rabbi Eliezer raised his arms and exclaimed, "Woe is me. For these two arms are like two Torah Scrolls and must now leave this world. If all the seas were ink and all the reeds were pens and all men were scribes they could not write down all that I have learned in Bible, and in Mishnah and all that I learned from my teachers. Yet I took from them no more that a man who dips his finger in the sea, and my disciples took from me no more than the paint-brush takes from its tube!"

Rabbi Eleazar ben Azariah then asked him a question and he pronounced his decision, "*It is clean*" and died with those words on his lips, Rabbi Eleazar tore his garments, wept and announced to the waiting sages, "My masters! Come and see

Rabbi Eliezer who is clean for the world-to-come." After the Sabbath,[27] Rabbi Akiva met the bier of Rabbi Eliezer as it was being carried to the town of Lod for his burial and he proclaimed over it the eulogy of the prophet Elisha for his master, Elijah, "My father! My father! Chariot of Israel and its horsemen. (2 Kings 11:12). I have many coins (questions) but there is no banker to change them (i.e., to supply the answers)."

When Rabbi Eliezer had left his father's house to study Torah in Jerusalem, his brothers persuaded their father, Hyrcanus, to disinherit him and to this end Hyrcanus came to Jerusalem.[28] When Rabban Johanan ben Zakkai heard that Hyrcanus was coming he instructed the ushers to make sure to seat him in the front row at the academy and appointed Rabbi Eliezer to deliver the lecture that day. The latter was exceedingly apprehensive and refused on the grounds that if he spoke in the presence of his teacher he would deserve death. In this Rabbi Eliezer was consistent with his own opinion[29] that Nadav and Avihu, the two sons of Aaron the High Priest, were struck down by the Almighty because they handed down a decision in the presence of their elders, i.e., Moses and Aaron (Leviticus 10:1-3).

Rabban Johanan and the other members of the academy, however, insisted. According to one version, Rabban Johanan left - or made as if to leave - the study hall for the lecture. Be that as it may, Rabbi Eliezer's lecture was so illuminating that his face glowed and it was impossible to tell whether it was day or night. Rabban Johanan became so enthusiastic that he kissed Rabbi Eliezer on his forehead. Hyrcanus, at seeing the great honor in which his son was held, then rose and declared that he had come to Jerusalem to disinherit his son, but now he intended to disinherit all his other children and leave everything to Eliezer. Eliezer refused. "Had I wanted wealth," he said, "I had it. All I ever wanted was to study Torah which, thanks to the Almighty, I have merited to achieve!"

Notes

1. *Avot* 2:15
2. *Avot D'Rabbi Natan* 6:3; the story given here is according to this source. There are other versions.
3. *Pirkei D'Rabbi Eliezer* 7
4. *Avot* 2:11
5. *Ibid* 2:12
6. *TJ Avodah Zarah* 3:1
7. *Sukkah* 28a
8. *Gittin* 56a
9. *Avot* 2:13-14
10. *Ibid*, 2:15
11. *Berakhot* 28b
12. *Bava Metzia* 59a/b
13. *TJ Moed Katan* 3:1; *Bava Metzia* 59b
14. *Megilah* 3a
15. *TJ Pesahim* 6:3
16. *Sanhedrin* 68a; *TH Sanhedrin* 7:13; *Avot D'Rabbi Natan* 3:6
17. *Ta'anit* 25b
18. *Ibid*
19. *Avot* 2:15
20. *Ibid*
21. *Sanhedrin* 32b
22. *Midrash Rabbah,* Song of Songs 1:3:1
23. *Sanhedrin* 101a
24. *Ibid*, 68a
25: In the version of this incident given in *Avot D'Rabbi Natan* 25:3, 27a it is Rabbi Eliezer himself who gives this answer.
26. *Avot D'Rabbi Natan* 25:3 27a
27. *Sanhedrin* 68a
28. *Avot D'Rabbi Natan* 6:3 20b
29. *Yoma* 53a

Rabbi Tarfon

רַבִּי טַרְפוֹן אוֹמֵר: הַיּוֹם קָצָר וְהַמְּלָאכָה מְרֻבָּה, וְהַפּוֹעֲלִים
עֲצֵלִים, וְהַשָּׂכָר הַרְבֵּה, וּבַעַל הַבַּיִת דּוֹחֵק.

*Rabbi Tarfon said: "The day is short, and the work is great,
and the workmen are lazy, and the reward is much and the
Master is insistent."[1] He used to say: "You are not called
upon to complete the work but you are also not free to evade
it. If you have studied much Torah, they will give you much
reward and your Employer can be trusted to pay you for
your work. But realize that the reward of the righteous will
be given in the Time-to-Come."[2]*

In fixing the sequence of the *mishnayot*, Rabbi Judah the Nasi
properly placed Rabbi Tarton's *mishnah* after the statement of
Rabbi Eleazar,[3] for two reasons. Rabbi Eleazar had ended his
mishnah with the exhortation: "Know before whom you toil
and who your Employer is, who will pay you the reward for
your labor." Rabbi Tarfon's homily is also based on the
parable of workmen and their Employer.

The second reason has to do with the general order of the
mishnayot in Avot. In Chapter 1,[4] Rabbi Judah the Nasi
indicated the correct sequence of Israel's leaders from Moses
down to his own father, Rabban Simeon ben Gamaliel, with
whose dictum the chapter ended. Rabbi Judah then began
Chapter 2[5] with his own statement and that of his son, Rabban
Gamaliel III. He then reverted to Hillel and continued with
Rabban Johanan ben Zakkai and his five outstanding pupils.
After citing their dicta he then inserted Rabbi Tarfon,[6] who

was also a student of Rabban Johanan ben Zakkai but was too young to be included in the list of outstanding disciples. It must, however, be remembered that Rabbi Tarfon too was a great scholar as was indicated by Rabbi Dosa ben Hyrcanus who testified: "When Rabbi Tarfon was still a lad it was quite evident that he would be a scholar."[7]

Rabbi Tarfon was a *kohen*,[8] a priest, from his mother's side as well as his father's, of which fact he was quite proud, and had actually officiated in the Temple. He recalled that once he had ascended the dais to perform the *Birkat Kohanim,* the Priestly Blessing, together with his mother's brother. When he officiated as the *kohen* in the *Pidyon Ha-Ben* ceremony in which the male first-born is redeemed, Rabbi Tarfon often returned the five silver selas he received to the child's father because he knew that the financial position of most people at that time was very strained.[9]

Rabbi Tarfon was a great scholar and many farmers chose to give him the *Terumah*, the first tithe of their produce which had to be given to a *kohen*. Thus he received a great deal of produce. The law of *Terumah* is, that it can be eaten only by priests, their immediate families and their slaves and that it must be consumed in a state of ritual purity. Rabbi Tarfon "married" some three hundred women in order to enable them to eat the *Terumah* he received, and thus he alleviated their economic difficulties.[10]

Rabbi Tarfon was a witness to the destruction of the Second Temple and the massacres that came in its aftermath. He saw the great numbers of prisoners that were taken to be sold as slaves in Rome and throughout the Roman empire. How he himself escaped is not known but eventually we hear of him in Yavneh. He established his own Torah academy in the town of Lod but frequently travelled to Yavneh to participate in the discussions in the academy there and in the formulation of the law. In some discussions, he is recorded as the first spokesman. It seems that he was often given this honor, perhaps because of his priestly status. We read[11] that when he visited the ailing Rabbi Eliezer ben Hyrcanus together with three other sages, he was the first to speak and on that occasion, said to Rabbi Eliezer, "You are more important to Israel than rain, for rain is precious in this world, while your value is for this world and the next."

The war against the Romans devastated Eretz Israel and in its wake came economic disaster. The number of students at the Torah academies decreased drastically and, except for the academy at Yavneh and those in a few isolated towns, Torah study, to a great extent, virtually ceased. Rabbi Tarfon subscribed wholeheartedly to the philosophy of his teacher, Rabban Johanan ben Zakkai, that the survival of the Jewish people did not depend on the Temple but on the study of Torah and so he counselled the people: " life is short and the work (i.e., Torah study for the sake of Jewish survival) is great, ... You are not called upon to complete the work (i.e., not everybody can become as great a scholar as Rabbi Akiva) but you are also not free to evade it(i.e., you must study to the best of your ability)." He also reassured his listeners that each one would receive his just reward - not according to the amount of material he had mastered but according to the effort that he had invested in his studies.

On the subject of the importance of Torah study, Rabbi Tarfon seemed to contradict himself. His most devoted colleague was the great Rabbi Akiva with whom he is quoted in discussion more than with any other sage. A crucial quesstion was raised in the academy: What is more important - the study of Torah or the performance of the *mitzvot*? In the report of the discussion in the Babylonian Talmud[12] Rabbi Akiva ruled that study is more important while Rabbi Tarfon took the opposite view, i.e., that deeds are more important. Rabbi Tarfon's opinion seems to be consistent with another view he held, "No man dies except out of idleness!"[13] However, another source[14] cites Rabbi Tarfon as having ruled that study is more important and it was Rabbi Akiva who took the opposite position! Incidentally, when the academy voted on this issue, the majority decided that study was more important because it leads to the performance of deeds.

The contradiction between these two sources can be solved in a manner the Talmud itself uses on many occasions, i.e., "reverse the names" in one of the sources. However, it is possible to reconcile the sources without resorting to amending the text. There is a time for everything. We read in the Book of Psalms (119:126): "It is time to do for the Lord; they have made Your Torah void!" which is interpreted to mean that there are times when the study of Torah must be set aside in order to "do deeds." An example of this is, that even a group which is studying Torah must stop when the congregation is about to recite the *Shema* and join them in affirming the Almighty's unity and sovereignty.[15] An individual must also interrupt his studies when the time for reciting *Shema* arrives. Thus, there are times when deeds are more important than study.

Rabbi Tarfon certainly practiced what he preached. Once, he was sitting and teaching his students when a bridal procession passed by. He immediately interrupted his lecture and instructed his mother and his wife to bathe and annoint the bride and dance before her all the way to her bridegroom's house.[16]

As had been predicted in his childhood, Rabbi Tarfon became an outstanding scholar.[17] He was described as a "heap of nuts." Just as when you remove one nut from a heap the others roll off, so too Rabbi Tarfon - when you asked him a question, answers began to roll off his tongue quoting Scripture, *Mishnah, Halakhah* and *Aggadah*. When a student left Rabbi Tarfon's presence he departed laden with spiritual and intellectual wealth.

Rabbi Tarfon was in the habit of emphasizing his point of view by using the expression, "May I lose my children if this is not so..."[18] Although this was only a habit of speech, "wise men must be careful of their words!" And so we are told[19] that when Rabbi Judah the Nasi visited the town of Lod where Rabbi Tarfon had lived he asked the people, "Has that righteous man who used to swear by his children's lives left a son?" "No," they replied, "but he has left a grandson by his daughter." This grandson was a profligate and Rabbi Judah persuaded him to repent his evil ways. One cannot help thinking that Rabbi Tarfon would have been better advised to find a different expression to stress his opinion.

Notwithstanding his seniority among the sages, Rabbi Tarfon was never ashamed to ask his colleagues when he did not understand the law.[20] In one instance he exclaimed: "May I lose my children if I did not hear that there is a difference between the acceptance of the blood and its sprinkling in the performance of a sacrifice, but I cannot explain it."[21] (It should be remembered that he was a *kohen* who had actually served in the Temple). Rabbi Akiva explained the difference. Rabbi Tarfon then said: "By the holy Temple service! I heard there was a difference but could not explain it. You deduced it by logic exactly according to the tradition... Akiva! Whoever departs from you departs from life itself."

In Jerusalem Talmud[22] Rabbi Tarfon is described as "the father of all Israel, in learning "yet he made a mistake in ruling that a maimed *kohen* may sound the *shofar* over a sacrifice. He said: "May I lose my children if I did not see my lame uncle sounding the *shofar* in the Temple." Again, Rabbi Akiva set the situation aright by suggesting that, that had been at the Hakhel ceremony held once every seven years during the Sukkot festival. His memory so prodded, Rabbi Tarfon exclaimed, "Akiva, I saw it but forgot the exact circumstances, while you deduced it by logic. Akiva, whoever departs from you departs from life itself."

It would appear that Rabbi Tarfon's memory deteriorated with advancing age which is a common phenomenon. That is why he said on several occasions "I witnessed the event but cannot remember the exact circumstances" or "I heard the law from my teachers but cannot remember the explanation." To forget because of aging is no sin according to Rabbi Dostai[23] who quotes Rabbi Meir: "Scripture regards a person who forgets even one word of his learning as if he had forfeited his life... But he is not guilty until he deliberately removes his learning from his heart (i.e., deliberately forgets his learning)."

On a number of occasions, Rabbi Tarfon's conscience bothered him because of mistaken rulings he had handed down, as a result of his impaired memory. A question was asked regarding the *kashrut* of a cow that had had its womb removed surgically.[24] Rabbi Tarfon was not aware that this was a practice in Egypt and that the sages there had ruled such cows to be kosher. He ruled that it was not kosher. When the same question was asked at the academy, the sages ruled that such an animal is kosher and Rabbi Tarfon wanted to make restitution to the person whose cow he wrongly declared to be *treifah*. Rabbi Akiva calmed him by saying, "You are an expert judge, and you are entitled to your own opinion. Even when you err, you are not required to make restitution." No wonder that Rabbi Tarfon said of Rabbi Akiva that he revealed things that were hidden from human beings.[25]

Rabbi Tarfon was very sensitive about taking advantage of his status as a scholar.[26] Once, after the date harvest, he chanced on a palm plantation and picked up some of the fruit that had been left over and ate it. He was spotted by the watchman who, not knowing who he was, grabbed him put him in a sack and was about to throw him in the river. Rabbi Tarfon started shouting, "Woe to Rabbi Tarfon who is about to be murdered!" Hearing the name, Tarfon, the watchman dropped the sack and ran away. Rabbi Tarfon suffered severe pangs of conscience over this incident because he felt that he should have told the watchman that what is left over after the harvest and packing, may be taken and eaten by anybody or, alternatively, he should have offered payment. He should not

have used his fame as a scholar even to save himself. Did not
Hillel say,[27] "Whoever derives benefit from words of Torah,
takes his life out of this world!"

On the question of the credibility of evil rumors, Rabbi
Tarfon also exhibited great sensitivity.[28] A group of Galileans,
about whom it was rumored that they had committed murder,
came to Rabbi Tarfon and begged him to hide them. Rabbi
Tarfon was in a dilemma: Perhaps I should hide them because
it is only a rumor, and if they did not do the deed and are killed
by the murdered party's kinsmen, I will have been responsible
for shedding innocent blood. But if they are guilty and I hide
them, I will be a party to obstructing justice. Undecided, he
told the Galileans to hide elsewhere.

In his youth, Rabbi Tarfon had been very careful to fulfil the
dictum, "be as meticulous in the performance of a light
mitzvah as in a serious one."[29] The sages of the Talmud
interpreted "a light *mitzvah*" as the law that you send the
mother bird away before taking her eggs or her young
(Deuteronomy 22:6-7(and "a serious one" as the
commandment to honor one's parents (Exodus 20:12;
Deuteronomy 5:16). With regard to the latter *mitzvah* Rabbi
Tarfon was exceedingly meticulous and the Talmud records[30]
that when his mother wanted to enter or leave her bed, he
would bend down for her to step on his back. When he boasted
of this in the academy, his colleagues rebuked him: "You have
not yet reached a half of the honor due to her." When he fell
ill,[31] his mother came to the academy to ask his colleagues to
pray for his recovery and she too boasted of her son's piety in
honoring her. Once again the rabbis retorted that as much as he
had done he had not done even a half of what is required by the
mitzvah of honoring one's parents.

The Talmud relates an incident concerning Rabbi Tarfon
and Rabbi Akiva which ended with the former kissing the latter
and exclaiming: "My teacher! My master! My teacher in
wisdom! My master in good deeds!" Although he was the

senior, Rabbi Tarfon was humble enough to recognize the brilliance and scholarly superiority of his younger colleague.[33] Rabbi Akiva reciprocated this love and respect and was always exceedingly careful not to hurt Rabbi Tarfon's feelings even when he was correcting him. On one occasion,[34] Rabbi Tarfon was asked a question but could not answer, so he remained silent. Rabbi Judah ben Nehemiah, who was present, answered and still Rabbi Tarfon remained silent. Rabbi Judah's face lit up with joy at having been able to answer a question which had stumped Rabbi Tarfon. Rabbi Akiva remarked angrily: "Are you happy that you have refuted the old sage?! I doubt whether you will live long." Within nine weeks Rabbi Judah ben Nehemiah was dead.

The sources are not clear about Rabbi Tarfon's own death. According to the *Midrash*[35] he was one of the Ten Martyrs cruelly put to death by the Romans, but in the account of that tragedy we recite on Yom Kippur and Tisha Be-Av his name does not appear. In fact the *Midrash* itself cites a tradition that Rabbi Eleazar Harsena should be substituted for Rabbi Tarfon. If he was one of the Ten Martyrs, can we not question the justice of it? After all, did he not study Torah, perform *mitzvot*, distribute charity and exhort everyone to do the same? The answer is: Yes, but not enough according to his capacity and also not on his own initiative, but only on Rabbi Akiva's urging. Did he himself not say: The day is short, and the work is great, and the workmen are lazy?

It all adds up to one everlasting, universal truth. Do as much good as you can every day - tomorrow may be too late.

Notes

1. *Avot* 2:20
2. *Ibid*, 2:21
3. *Ibid*, 2:21

4. *Ibid*, 1:1
5. *Ibid*, 2:1
6. *Ibid*, 2:20
7. *TJ Yevamot* 1:6
8. *Kiddushim* 71a
9. *Bekhorot* 51b
10. *TJ Yevamot* 4:12
11. *Sanhedrin* 101a
12. *Kiddushin* 40b
13. *Avot D'Rabbi Natan* 11:1 - 22b
14. *Mekhilta Kedushin* 40
15. *Shabbat* 11a
16. *Avot D'Rabbi Natan* 41:13 - 34b
17. *Gittin* 67a; *Avot D'Rabbi Natan* 18:1 - 25a
18. *Shabbat* 17a, et al *TJ Yoma* 1:1
19. *Bava Metzia* 85a
20. *Bezah* 27b
21. *Zevahim* 13a
22. *TJ Yoma* 1:1
23. *Avot* 3:10
24. *Bekoroth* 28b
25. *Avot D'Rabbi Natan* 6:2 - 20b
26. *Nedarim* 62a
27. *Avot* 4:7
28. *Niddah* 61a
29. *Avot* 2:1
30. *Kiddushin* 31b
31. *TJ Peah* 1:1
32. *Midrash Rabbah, Leviticus* 34:16 - *Kallah Rabbathi* 52b
33. *Sanhedrin* 33a
34. *Menahot* 68b
35. *Midrash Rabbah, Lamentations* 2:4

Rabbi Simeon bar Yohai

רַבִּי שִׁמְעוֹן אוֹמֵר: שְׁלֹשָׁה שֶׁאָכְלוּ עַל שֻׁלְחָן אֶחָד וְלֹא אָמְרוּ
עָלָיו דִּבְרֵי תוֹרָה, כְּאִלּוּ אָכְלוּ מִזִּבְחֵי מֵתִים, שֶׁנֶּאֱמַר: כִּי כָל
שֻׁלְחָנוֹת מָלְאוּ קִיא צֹאָה בְּלִי מָקוֹם: אֲבָל שְׁלֹשָׁה שֶׁאָכְלוּ עַל
שֻׁלְחָן אֶחָד וְאָמְרוּ עָלָיו דִּבְרֵי תוֹרָה, כְּאִלּוּ אָכְלוּ מִשֻּׁלְחָנוֹ שֶׁל
מָקוֹם, שֶׁנֶּאֱמַר: וַיְדַבֵּר אֵלַי, זֶה הַשֻּׁלְחָן אֲשֶׁר לִפְנֵי יהוה:

*Rabbi Simeon (bar Yohai) said: If three men have eaten at a
table and have not spoken words of Torah, it is as though
they had eaten of sacrifices offered to the dead as it is
written: "For all their tables are full of vomit and filth. The
All-Present is not there!" (Isaiah 28:8). But if three eat at
table and do speak words of Torah, it is as though they had
eaten at the table of the All-Present as it is written: "And He
spoke to me: This (the altar in the Temple which was three
cubits high and thus evocative of the three men who eat
together) is the table which is before God" (Ezekiel 41:22).[1]*

It was Rabbi Simeon's custom to explain the laws or statements
of the sages by using a special formula: "Why is the law thus?
because..." or "What are the reasons for this scriptural injuc-
tion? because..." A good example of his didactic system is:
"Why did the High Priest not wear his golden robes when he
entered the Holy of Holies (on Yom Kippur)? because the
prosecuting counsel gold (which was used to make the Golden
calf) cannot be a defending counsel."[2] In discussing Rabbi
Simeon's various statements, it is surely only fitting that we
follow his example.

Rabbi Simeon took pains to teach his son good manners: "Do not enter your own house without knocking; and how much more so does this apply to a neighbor's house."[3] The Talmud[4] tells us the story of Rabbi Hanania ben Hakinai who, immediately after his wedding went off with Rabbi Simeon to study at the academy of Rabbi Akiva. He stayed there for 13 years and did not keep in touch with his home. Rabbi Simeon, however, was assiduous in maintaining contact with his home, and would regularly send his wife messages inquiring of her welfare and reporting his own progress in his studies. One day, Hanania heard that his daughter was about to be married and decided to surprise his wife by going home to attend the wedding. His wife received such a shock at his unexpected appearance that she fainted and only Hanania's prayers saved her from death. Surely, this incident was what motivated Rabbi Simeon to instruct his son to knock before entering and not surprise people!

In the same vein, we can ask: Why did Rabbi Simeon use the verse from Isaiah, "For all their tables are full of vomit and filth," as his source?[4] Because Rabbi Simeon was well aware of the disgusting Roman custom of guests making themselves vomit at a meal so that they would be able to eat more! In another instance, Rabbi Simeon expanded his aphorism: "A scholar must not participate in any banquet which is not of a religious nature."[5]

Under the Roman occupation of Eretz Israel, many scholars left the country in order to continue their Torah studies and practice their faith openly. Torah and Judaism were proscribed by the Roman administration and those sages who did remain in Eretz Israel studied by themselves, or, at the most, in secret with a colleague. "Two are company; three is a crowd," goes the popular adage and indeed if three were to study Torah in those days it would soon have become public knowledge with tragic consequences. Rabbi Simeon was not afraid of these consequences and wanted to encourage others to study Torah -

even in large groups. He was convinced that the Jewish People can survive only through the study of Torah. Thus he taught: "If *three* eat at a table and do speak words of Torah..."

Rabbi Simeon was perhaps the most extreme of the sages in his hatred of the Romans. He could find nothing good in them. It is related[6] that on one occasion he was sitting with his colleagues, Rabbi Judah and Rabbi Jose, discussing the Romans. Rabbi Judah praised the Roman administration: "How fine are the deeds of this (the Roman) people! They build markets; they build bridges; they build public bath-houses." Rabbi Jose prudently remained silent but Rabbi Simeon could not control himself: "Whatever they do, they do for their own benefit. They only build market places so that the prostitutes will have somewhere to ply their trade; they only build bridges so as to collect tolls, and they only build bath-houses in order to pamper themselves."

One, Judah ben Gerim, (Proselytes), was present during this dialogue and repeated this conversation which reached the ears of the authorities, thus expressing the danger of "three sitting together." The Romans showed honor to Rabbi Judah, who had praised them; exiled Rabbi Jose, who had remained silent; and sentenced Rabbi Simeon to death.

Simeon, and his son Eleazar escaped and hid in a cave for 12 years. A carob tree grew up miraculously in fromt of the entrance to the cave thus concealing their hiding place and supplying them with food at the same time. A stream also miraculously appeared so they had water to drink and to wash themselves. It was presumably this experience which led Rabbi Simeon to say: "When Israel performs the will of God, their work is done for them by others as it is written, '...strangers shall stand and feed your flock' (Isaiah 61:5)."[7]

Rabbi Simeon and his son did not waste the time they spent in hiding. Stripped naked, they sat covered with sand up to their necks and studied Torah day and night. When it was time to pray, they dressed and recited their prayers. Then, back to the sand pits and their studies! They followed this routine so that their clothes would not wear out. It is thought that one of the results of their long stay in the cave was the *Zohar*, "Book of Splendor," the mystical commentary *par excellence* on the Torah which Rabbi Simeon wrote. (There are some philosophers however who negate this thought). This work is the basic text for the study of *Kabbalah*.

When they finally left their hiding place, they were met by Simeon's son-in-law, Rabbi Phinhas ben Yair, who burst into tears upon seeing their emaciated condition and the sores which had covered their bodies. "Woe to me that I see you in such a state!" "On the contrary," said his father-in-law, "for if you did not see me in this condition, you would not find so much knowledge in me." Before he had gone into hiding, when Rabbi Simeon asked Rabbi Phinhas a question, the latter would give him thirteen answers. Now the tables were turned! Rabbi Simeon answered Rabbi Phinhas' questions with twenty-four explanations!

The Talmud[8] records the following conversation between Rabbi Simeon bar Yohai and his teacher, Rabbi Akiva. The latter was in prison for teaching Torah in contravention of the Hadrianic decrees which forbade the practice of Judaism. Simeon visited him and requested that he teach him Torah. Rabbi Akiva refused to comply because he did not want to endanger the life of his favorite pupil. Simeon threatened Rabbi Akiva, that if he refused him, he would tell his father, Yohai, who would persuade the authorities to withdraw the privileges that Rabbi Akiva enjoyed even in prison. Simeon's father, Yohai, was known to be what one would refer to today as "a dove" in his attitude to the Roman occupation. He felt that Rome was too mighty for the small Judea to have any chance of success in a revolt. His outlook was known to the Romans who showed him favor for it.

In contrast to his father, Simeon hated the Romans with burning passion, as we have noted above. Apparently, Yohai used his connections with the Romans—presumably bribery—to make Rabbi Akiva's incarceration more bearable. He was allowed to have one of his students, Judah Hagarsi, in attendance to bring him water and look after his needs. Rabbi Simeon could visit him for lessons in Torah and even the Roman governor came to debate with him.[9] Rabbi Simeon bar Yohai was most probably threatening his teacher that unless he taught him, his father would arrange to have Rabbi Akiva's privileges cancelled. Rabbi Akiva gave in to Rabbi Simeon and said, "More than the calf wants to suck (i.e, student to learn), the cow wants to suckle (i.e., the teacher wants to teach)."

Rabbi Simeon was a very independent and outspoken person and even disagreed with Rabbi Akiva when he thought his teacher was wrong. On the interpretation of the verse in the Book of Zechariah (8:19) dealing with the fast days, Rabbi Simeon said bluntly: "Rabbi Akiva gave four interpretations but I do not interpret like him!"[10] On another occasion, Rabbi Simeon told his students: "My sons, follow my rules, for they are the selected essence of Rabbi Akiva's teachings."[11]

Rashi, citing *Avot D'Rabbi Natan*,[12] describes Rabbi Akiva's career as a student and as a teacher in a very picturesque manner. "To what could Rabbi Akiva be compared? To a poor man who takes his box and goes out into the fields. If he finds barley, he reaps it and puts it into his box; if he finds wheat he takes it and throws it in his box; and the same with beans and lentils. When he arrives home, he sorts out all the different kinds he has gathered. So too Rabbi Akiva. When he had studied with his teachers he heard *Bible, Halakhah* (law) and *Aggadah* (lore) and reviewed his studies without putting the information into categories. But when he became a great scholar he sorted everything out and taught the knowledge to his students in categories..." Apparently, Rabbi Simeon went even further and discarded all the extraneous material, teaching his students only the essential law. That is why he told them to follow his rules.

your Creator and I know your capacity," (but according to the Penei Moshe a commentator on the Jerusalem Talmud) Meir is older![13] Simeon, together with Meir and three other scholars, was ordained by Rabbi Judah ben Bava. In that list of five, Rabbi Simeon is listed third.[14]

Such was Rabbi Simeon bar Yohai's love of Torah that he would say: "Three things were given to Israel but only through great suffering - Torah, the Land of Israel, and the World to Come."[15] It is this thought that offers an explanation of what is otherwise an extraordinary statement of Rabbi Simeon's: "I am able to exempt the whole world from judgement from the day I was born until now. Were Eleazar, my son, with me, we could exempt the world from judgement from the day of creation until now. And were Yotham the son of Uzziah with us, we could exempt it from the day of creation until the end of time."[16] Was Rabbi Simeon so vain as to believe that his merit was so great? Could a student of Rabbi Akiva seriously believe that about himself?

The answer is to be found in Rabbi Simeon's previous aphorism. He had suffered unbearably for 12 years for the sake of Torah and in order to stay in Eretz Israel. He had acquired Torah and Eretz Israel through suffering and therefore he had a right to the third gift, the World to Come, i.e., exemption from judgement. His personal suffering had been so great that he could absolve the whole world from its wrong-doings. However, why did he include Yotham the son of Uzziah? Rashi explains that Yotham was a most righteous and humble person. He ruled as regent while his father, King Uzziah, was stricken with leprosy, yet he never attempted to usurp the throne and never gave a ruling without quoting his father as the source. Of Yotham it was said: "A son gives honor to his father" (Malachi 1:6). Of interest is the fact that Rashi's commentary of Chronicles (2-27:2) lists the sins of each and every king except Yotham, who was blameless. With such a partner, Simeon and his son Eleazar could truly have saved the world![17]

Another example of Rabbi Simeon's apparent vanity is the following:"Hezekiah said in the name of Rav Jeremiah who said in the name of Rabbi Simeon bar Yohai: I have seen the sons of heaven (i.e., those who will go to paradise) and they are few. If there are a thousand, I and my son are among them. If a hundred, I and my son are among them. And if there are only two, they are my son and I."[18]

This too is an extraordinary statement. But if we consider the circumstances, we may be able to understand it a little better. Judaism was proscribed and Jews were afraid to study *Torah* or practice their faith for fear of being caught and executed. Rabbi Simeon wanted to encourage people to study Torah and observe the *mitzvot* notwithstanding the Romans. He therefore emphasized that there are only a limited number of souls in *Gan Eden* and that these would be of the people who studied Torah and kept *mitzvot* through suffering, just as he and his son Eleazar had done.

Rabbi Simeon felt very strongly about the unity of the Jewish People and the responsibility of each Jew for the fate of the entire nation. "If one Jew sins, all Israel feels it,"[19] was one of his aphorisms which he illustrated with the following parable, which, to most people, is not associated with Rabbi Simeon: "This may be compared to the case of a man in a boat who began boring a hole under his seat. The other travellers tried to stop him but he insisted: 'It's none of your business! I am boring under my own seat.' "Yes", they answered, 'but the water (the bad reputation caused by sin) will affect us all.'

Nothwithstanding his mysticism and his incredible suffering, Rabbi Simeon exhibited great humaneness—and astuteness — in many of his decisions. The following is a prime example:[20] A couple once came before Rabbi Simeon in order to be divorced. They had been married for ten years without offspring and in law this is considered sufficient grounds for divorce. Rabbi Simeon suggested that just as they had been married with a joyous celebration and a banquet, so they should be divorced with a banquet before the divorce ceremony. The couple went along with the idea and made a party to which they invited their friends. At the party, the husband told his wife that she could take anything she wanted with her when she returned to her father's house. The lady saw to it that her husband became very drunk and when he passed out she had him taken to her father's house. When he woke up bewildered he asked, "What am I doing here?" "You told me that I could take anything I wanted," she replied. "Well, I want you!" The couple returned to Rabbi Simeon to report the strange outcome of his suggestion. He prayed for them and they were blessed with children.

Rabbi Siemon had great respect for physical labor and used to say, "Great is labor, for it honors he who performs it." He even went to the extent of demonstratively carrying a basket on his shoulders.[21] Yet, on the other hand, the law that scholars engaged in study must interrupt their studies for the recitation of the *Shema* but not for the statutory prayers, was explained by Rabbi Johanan as referring only to such scholars as Rabbi Simeon bar Yohai and his companions "for whom study is their profession."[22]

This apparent contradiction can be reconciled on a chronological basis. The first statement was made before Simeon's experience in the cave. His attitude then was what may be called "normative rabbinic." After his years in the cave, however, his whole attitude changed. From then on, the study of Torah was all that mattered, and Rabbi Johanan's remark referred to that particular period.

Indeed, the Talmud records[23] that when Simeon and Eleazar emerged from the cave, they saw a farmer attending to his field and were unable to understand how a person could do anything but study Torah: "They forsake life eternal and engage in life temporal!" At this remark, a heavenly voice ordered them back into the cave for another 12 months. When they emerged the second time they met a man hurrying along carrying two bunches of myrtle sprigs.

"What are they for?" they asked.

"In honor of the Sabbath (for their frangrance)," he replied.

"But why two bunches?"

One is for 'Remember the Sabbath day' (Exodus 20:8) and the other is for 'Observe the Sabbath day' (Deuteronomy 5:12)."

Thus, Rabbi Simeon and his son Eleazar realized that even the Jews' "temporal life" is for the sake of "life eternal."

Gratitude was another of Rabbi Simeon's great characteristics. When he and Eleazar came out of hiding they were in poor physical condition. Their bodies were covered with sores and blisters as a result of sitting in the sand up to their necks for so long a period of time. They went for a period of treatment to the hot mineral springs of Tiberias, (which are still famous for their therapeutic powers) and were eventually cured. Rabbi Eleazar then said to his father, "These waters have healed us. Should we not do something for the community to show our gratitude?"

The town of Tiberias had been built by King Herod in honor of the Roman emperor, Tiberius. He had built it on the site of a cemetery with the result that *kohanim* and other pious Jews who were concerned with ritual purity, could not live there. Indeed, the town was populated by a "mixed multitude."[24] Rabbi Simeon undertook the major task of locating and removing the graves as an act of gratitude for being cured by the waters of Tiberias.[25]

All in all, more than 300 laws are quoted in Rabbi Simeon's name in the Talmud and, in addition to the *Zohar,* he edited the *Sifrei* and the *Mekhilta,* two of the most important works of the halakhic *midrashim.*

Simeon bar Yohai is buried in Meron in the Galilee and his grave is one of the main centers of Jewish pilgrimage. He died on Lag Ba-Omer, the 33rd day of the Counting of the Omer between Passover and Shavuot, and that day is still observed by tens of thousands who come to Meron to celebrate the *Hilula D'Rabbi Simeon bar Yohai,* the anniversary of Rabbi Simeon's pure soul's ascension to heaven.

Notes

1. *Avot* 3:4
2. *Midrash Rabbah, Leviticus* 21:10
3. *Ibid,* 21:8
4. *Ketubbot* 62b *Ibid* 21:8
5. *Pesahim* 49a
6. *Shabbat* 33b
7. *Berakhot* 35b
8. *Pesahim* 112a
9. *Sanhedrin* 65b
10. *Rosh HaShanah* 18b
11. *Gittin* 67a
12. *Avot D'Rabbi Natan* 18:1 25a/b
13. *TJ Sanhedrin* 1:2
14. *Sanhedrin* 14a
15. *Sifrei, Ekev* 32
16. *Sukkah* 45b
17. I am indebted to Ha-Rav Hagaon Rabbi Abraham Kroll of Jerusalem, for this insight.
18. *Sifrei, Ekev* 32
19. *Midrash Rabbah, Leviticus* 4:6
20. *Midrash Rabbah,* Song of Songs 1:4:2
21. *Nedarim* 49b
22. *Shabbat* 11a
23. *Shabbat* 33b
24. Josephus, *Antiquities* 18:2
25. *Midrash Rabbah, Genesis* 79:6

Rabbi Akiva ben Joseph

רַבִּי עֲקִיבָא אוֹמֵר: שְׂחוֹק וְקַלּוּת רֹאשׁ מַרְגִּילִין אֶת הָאָדָם
לְעֶרְוָה. מָסוֹרֶת סְיָג לַתּוֹרָה, מַעְשְׂרוֹת סְיָג לָעֹשֶׁר, נְדָרִים סְיָג
לַפְּרִישׁוּת, סְיָג לַחָכְמָה שְׁתִיקָה.

Rabbi Akiva said: Jesting and levity lead a man to lewdness.
The Massorah (the correct text of the Scriptures) is a fence
to the Torah. Tithes are a fence for wealth. Vows are a fence
for self-restraint. A fence for wisdom is silence.[1]

It is indeed remarkable that Rabbi Akiva, the descendant of
converts to Judaism, who only began to study Torah at the age
of 40,[2] could achieve so outstanding a reputation that Rabbi
Dosa could say of him: "Are you the Akiva ben Joseph whose
name is known from one end of the world to the other?"[3]

Rabbi Akiva's early history is shrouded in mystery. It is
thought that he was born in Upper Galilee. What is known is
that his father was a convert to Judaism who traced his
ancestry to Sisra, the general of the Canaanite king, Yavin
(Judges 4:2).[4] In two places in the Talmud,[5] it is recorded that
descendants of Sisra studied and taught Torah in Jerusalem
and this is understood to refer to Rabbi Akiva. We also know[6]
that Rabbi Akiva was an agricultural worker and that he was
employed in the vineyards of Rabbi Eliezer ben Hyrkanus for
three years. Thereafter he worked as a shepherd for Kalba
Savua and met the latter's daughter Rachel whom he married.

At one point during his career, he was a candidate to be
president of the Sanhedrin, but was denied the honor because
he was a descendant of converts and thus had no *yihus*, i.e., was

not of a distinguished lineage.[7] According to one source,[8] Akiva's father, Joseph, lived to enjoy his son's greatness.

Most people know of Rabbi Akiva from the stories about his death in the section on the Ten Martyrs that is read in the prayers of the 9th of Av and the additional service on Yom Kippur. Some know of him from Avot and others from his statements in the Talmud. Few people, however, associate his aphorisms with actual incidents that happened to him or his family.

In our *mishnah*, we read that the *Massorah*, the traditional correct text of the Bible, is a fence to the Torah, for it is only in accordance with that text that the Written Law can properly be expounded and interpreted. Thus Rabbi Akiva interpreted even the so-called "meaningless" words in the Torah such as "et" which is normally taken merely to be the sign of the grammatical objective case. Rabbi Akiva had been a student of Nahum Ish Gam Zu[9] and had learned this method of interpretation, from him. One good example of this method is the interpretation of the verse, "Honor *et* your father *v-et* your mother" (Exodus 20:12). The *et*, being superfluous is taken to mean that a step-father or step-mother must also be honored, as long as they are the spouse of a living natural parent, as must an elder brother.[10] Another example is the *et* in "You shall fear *et* the Lord, your God" (Deuteronomy 6:13) which is taken to include obedience to sages.[11]

On the verse, "This is the book of the generations of Adam" (Genesis 5:1) the Talmud states that God showed Adam all the generations and their scholars that would arise until the end of time. When Adam saw Rabbi Akiva he rejoiced at his erudition but was exceedingly grieved at his tragic death.[12] In a similar vein, the Talmud cites the following tradition: Rabbi Judah said in the name of Rav: "When Moses ascended on high to receive the Ten Commandments, he found the Holy One, Blessed be He, engaged in fixing crowns, *tagin* - ornamental risers from the tops of certain letters in the script used for writing Torah scrolls, to the letters of the Torah. Moses asked: 'Why the need for crowns?' to which the Almighty responded: 'In the future there will arise an individual, Akiva ben Joseph, who will expound heaps and heaps of laws on each crown." The Talmud continues that Moses asked to see this person. The Almighty told him to turn around, and Moses found himself sitting in the last row of a class in which Rabbi Akiva was expounding a law. To his chagrin, Moses did not understand the lecture at all and became increasingly confused until Rabbi Akiva said: "We have this law as one handed down by Moses from Sinai."

Moses was also shown Rabbi Akiva's tragic end, and when he complained to the Almighty, he was told: "Be silent! Such is My decree!"[13]

Giving tithes (i.e., sharing one's possessions) is a fence to wealth.[1]

When Rabbi Akiva was a penniless shepherd, he married Rachel. the daughter of Kalba Savua, a wealthy landowner, who objected to the match and disinherited his daughter. Akiva and Rachel lived in a hut and were so poor that their bed was a mere bundle of straw.[14] One day a man came to their door and begged for some straw for his wife who had just given birth. He was so poor that he could not even afford straw to sleep on. Akiva and Rachel gladly shared their straw with this stranger who was even more unfortunate than they were. The Talmud informs us that this stranger was none other than Elijah the Prophet who had come to test them. On that same page of Talmud, we are told how Rabbi Akiva ultimately became wealthy himself but used all his wealth for the benefit of his students and the poor.[15] He also acted as the treasurer of charity funds and even travelled to distant countries to raise money for the relief of the poor.

When Akiva left home to study, Rachel had to cut off her golden braids of hair and sell them in order to survive. When Rabbi Akiva became aware of what she had done he promised her that some day he would make her a "Jerusalem of Gold" which is explained to mean a golden tiara with the sky-line of Jerusalem engraved on it. And so he did.

Rabbi Akiva finally returned home after 24 years of study, he was accompanied by thousands of his students. Rachel pushed her way through the crowds that had come to welcome the great scholar, fell to her knees and kissed the hem of his tunic. When the students, who did not know her, tried to remove her, Rabbi Akiva stopped them: "Leave her! All the knowledge that I possess and all that you, my students have acquired, is hers."[14] He then gave her the Jerusalem of Gold that he had promised her. The Talmud records the following piquant conversation between Rabban Gamliel and his wife who were there:

"You never made me a tiara like that!" said his wife.

"Neither did you do the things she did!"[16] replied Rabban Gamliel.

In addition to the incidents describing how Rabbi Akiva became rich, the Gemara presents an illuminating picture of the meeting between the wealthy Kalba Savua and his son-in-law, Rabbi Akiva, the ignorant shepherd who had become the great sage.

Kalba Savua heard that a great Rabbi had come and visited him to see if he could get a release from his vow to disinherit his daughter Rachel.[17] Not recognizing the great and honored scholar as his former ignorant son-in-law, Kalba Savua told him his story and asked whether he could be released from the vow. Rabbi Akiva asked him a simple question: "If you had known that your son-in-law would become a scholar, would you have made that vow?" Kalba Savua replied: "If I had thought that he would even know a single verse or even one law, I would not have vowed." "You are released from your vow," said Rabbi Akiva, "I am your ignorant son-in-law." Kalba Savua later bestowed a great part of his fortune on his son-in-law who used it to support his students and the needy.

Rabbi Akiva's association with Tinius Rufus also had an interesting outcome.[18] The two, one the leading sage and the other the Roman governor of Judea, held many discussions but Tinius Rufus would always come away angry because he could never win an argument. On one occasion, Rabbi Akiva baited him cruelly and he returned to his residence in an extremely irate state of mind. His wife, Rufina, on hearing the cause of her husband's anger said, "The God of the Jews hates fornication, with your permission, I will go and tempt Rabbi Akiva into sin." Tinius Rufus consented to her plan and she set out bedecked on her mission. When Rabbi Akiva saw her he spat , wept, and smiled. She demanded an explanation and Rabbi Akiva told her that he had spat because such a beautiful creature as she came from a "malodorous drop (of semen)," that he had cried, because she, so beautiful, would rot in the earth like all mankind. He would tell her why he smiled "on another occasion." Rufina returned several times and continued her discussions with Rabbi Akiva until she converted to Judaism and ultimately married him as he had known she would. Thus the smile. Rufina brought him great wealth which was also used for charity.[19]

A fence to wisdom is silence.[1]

Rabbi Johanan ben Nuri said:[20] "I call Heaven to witness that more than five times I berated Rabbi Akiva in the presence of Rabban Gamliel but he responded with love to fulfill the verse 'Admonish the wise and they will love you for it' (Proverbs 9:8)."

Once when Rabbi Akiva was still a student, he was walking along a road and came across a dead body,. He carried it until he found a cemetery and buried it there, thinking that he had performed a great *mitzvah*. When he came to the *yeshivah* and told Rabbi Eliezer and Rabbi Joshua what he had done, they rebuked him saying: "A body found on the road must be buried at the spot where it was found." They also told him that he had committed a transgression with every step that he had taken with the corpse. Akiva did not try to justify his action; he had not known the law and remained silent vowing never to budge from the side of his teachers.[21]

Again we find Rabbi Akiva applying this philosophy of "a fence to wisdom is silence" in his own behavior. According to the Talmud,[22] Rabbi Akiva studied for 13 years at the academy of Rabbi Eliezer ben Hyrkanus and Rabbi Joshua, but he did not participate in any discussions because he believed that"when the Rabbi teaches, the students should sit and absorb." Indeed, during those years, Rabbi Eliezer paid very little attention to him. After all, Akiva had been a shepherd and had worked for Rabbi Eliezer as a laborer for three years prior to his starting his studies and, thus, not a great deal was expected of him. However, on one question, Rabbi Akiva offered an opinion that differed from his teacher's. Rabbi Joshua, in an allusion to Judges 9:38, then said to Rabbi Eliezer: "You ignored Rabbi Akiva all these years. Now go out and do battle with him!"

Of interest is the fact that in both the Babylonian and Jerusalem Talmuds, Rabbi Akiva is cited more than six hundred times in matters of law and lore, and the law goes according to his version in more than 350 cases!

> He (Rabbi Akiva) used to say: Everything is given on pledge, and a net is spread for all the living: the shop is open; and the store keeper gives credit; and the ledger lies open; and the hand writes; and whosoever wishes to borrow may come and borrow; but the collectors regularly make their daily round; and exact payment from man whether he be aware of it or not.[23]

From this powerful allegory, it would seem that Rabbi Akiva believed that "death never takes a holiday!" Yet in another statement he apparently takes the opposite view.[24] In a discussion of the verse, "but charity saves from death" (Proverbs 10:2) which the Rabbis explain as meaning a *painful* death, Rabbi Akiva differs and says that it means from death itself. In other words, it appears that Rabbi Akiva believed that death can be thwarted.

There is however, no contradiction. Rabbi Akiva believed that an unusual act of righteousness *can* save a person from death. And so it happened with his own daughter.[24]

It had been foretold that Rabbi Akiva's daughter would die on her wedding day, yet on the morning following the ceremony she was still alive. Rabbi Akiva, greatly surprised, asked her to tell him what she had done on her wedding day. As far as she could see nothing unusual had happened except that just before the wedding feast a poor man had come to the door begging for food. As everybody else was busy with the wedding banquet, she herself had served him of her own portion of food. At the same time she told her father that she had mislaid a gold necklace that he had given her. It was a gold pendant with needle-like projections. It was later found with one of these projections pierced through the eye of a poisonous snake.

Thus, all the statements were correct. Akiva's daughter had been destined to die on her wedding day. The collector (i.e., the snake) had been ready. But, because of her virtuous deed in feeding the poor man, she had been spared not only from a painful death but from death itself.

In *Avot D'Rabbi Natan*,[25] Rabbi Akiva told the following story: It once happened that a pious man, who was very generous in charitable affairs, was travelling on a ship that went down in a storm with all its passengers. Rabbi Akiva, who had witnessed the tragedy from the shore, was prepared to testify that he had seen the man drown - such testimony being essential to enable the widow to remarry. When the man himself later appeared, alive and well, Rabbi Akiva asked,

"Are you not the man who drowned?"

"Yes I am."

"How, then, were your saved?" asked Rabbi Akiva.

"While I was drowning, I heard one wave calling to another: 'Hurry, let us bring this man up from the sea

because he has dispensed charity all his life!"
On hearing this, Rabbi Akiva remarked: "The words of Torah endure forever! Cast your bread upon the water for you shall find it after many days (Ecclesiastes 11:1) and Charity saves from death (Proverbs 10:2)."

Rabbi Akiva's tragic death at the hands of the Romans together with nine other famous sages is well known.[26] The Romans tore his flesh with iron combs intent on inflicting as much pain and suffering as they could on this venerable sage who symbolized everything they hated. Rabbi Akiva accepted his suffering most probably repeating to himself the philosophy he had so often heard from his teacher, Nahum Ish Gamzu, "*Gam zu letovah*" - This, too, is for the good!

The time was the hour for the recitation of the *Shema* and when one of his anguished disciples said to him: "Our teacher! Even as much as this!?" Akiva replied: "All my days I have been troubled by the verse, 'Thou shalt love the Lord thy God with all thy heart, and with all thy soul and with all thy might' (Deuteronomy 6:5). 'With all thy heart' - I have fulfilled. 'With all thy might' which means possessions - I have also fulfilled. But I always wondered whether I would ever merit being able to fulfill 'With all thy soul' which means 'even if He takes thy soul.' Now I am able to perform this *Mitzvah* as well."

As he completed the *Shema*, Akiva ben Joseph's pure and virtuous soul ascended to heaven to receive its proper reward as he, Akiva, had taught: "and all is prepared for the banquet."[23]

The respect in which the former ignorant shepherd was held by his colleagues is clearly evident from the Talmud's evaluation of his death: When Rabbi Akiva died - the wells of Torah dried up![27]

Perhaps Rabbi Akiva's most famous aphorism is to be found in the following incident. Once Rabban Gamliel, Rabbi Eleazar, Rabbi Joshua and Rabbi Akiva went up to Jerusalem. When they came within sight of the destroyed and desolate

Temple Mount, they rent their garments as a sign of mourning as they were required to do by law. A fox ran out of the ruins that had been the Holy of Holies and the rabbis wept - except for Akiva who even seemed happy!

"Why do you smile?" they demanded.

"Why do you weep?" he replied.

"Of this place the Torah says 'The stranger who approaches shall be put to death! (Numbers 1:51), so holy is it, and now foxes run there! How can we not weep?"

"That is exactly why I smile," replied Akiva. "There are two prophecies about the Temple. The first is: 'Therefore, Zion shall be ploughed as a field' (Micah 3:12; Jeremiah 26:18) and the other is: 'Thus says the Almighty: Once again old men and women shall sit in the broad places of Jerusalem' (Zechariah 9:4). Until the first prophecy was fulfilled, I was afraid that perhaps the second would not. Now that I see the first prophecy fulfilled literally, I am sure that the second prophecy will one day come to pass!"

"Akiva, you have comforted us! Akiva, you have comforted us!"[28] replied his learned companions.

Our generation has begun to see the fulfillment of Rabbi Akiva's dream - so may it continue until we see the coming of the true Messiah, speedily in our day.

Notes

1. *Avot* 3:17
2. *Mamonodies Mishna Torah Intriduction—Avot D'Rabbi Natan*
3. *Yevamot* 160
4. *R. Nissim Gaon to Berakhot* 27b
5. *Sanhedrin* 96b. *Gittin* 57b:
6. *Sheiltot de Rav Aha Gaon, Sheiltot* 40
7. *Berakhot* 27b; *TJ Berakhot* 4:1
8. *Semahot* 8

9. *Berakhot* 22a
10. See Chapter 15 for Rabbi Judah H-Nasi's instructions to his sons. *Ketubot* 103a-TJ
11. *Pesahim* 22b
12. *Sanhedrin* 38b
13. *Menahot* 29b
14. *Nedarim* 50a/b
15. *Kiddushin* 272 *Ma'ser Sheni* 5:9
16. *TJ Shabbat* T.J.Sotah 9:15
17. *Ketuboth 63a*
18. *Rav to Nedarim* 50a
19. *Nedarim* 50b *Avodah Zarah* 20a
20. *Sifrei, Deuteronomy* 1 *Arakim* 16b
21. *TJ Nazir* 7:1
22. *Tj Pesahim* 6:3
23. *Avot* 3:20
24. *Shabbat* 156b
25. *Avot D'Rabbi Natan* 19b
26. *Berakhot* 61b
27. *TJ Sotah* 9:16
28. *Makkot* 24a/b

Rabbi Meir

רַבִּי מֵאִיר אוֹמֵר: אַל תִּסְתַּכֵּל בְּקַנְקַן, אֶלָּא בְּמַה שֶׁיֵּשׁ בּוֹ. יֵשׁ
קַנְקַן חָדָשׁ מָלֵא יָשָׁן, וְיָשָׁן שֶׁאֲפִילוּ חָדָשׁ אֵין בּוֹ.

*Rabbi Meir said: Do not pay attention to the flask but to
what its contents. Sometimes a new flask can be filled with
old wine, and sometimes an old flask can be empty even of
new wine.*[1]

Rabbi Meir is the fourth *tanna* in our study who was a
descendant of converts to Judaism. The other three were
Shemayah and Avtalyon,[2] and Rabbi Akiva.[3] According to the
Talmud, Rabbi Meir was a descendent of no less a figure than
the Emperor Nero.[4] His name was really Nehorai, but he was
called Meir because, he enlightened (Hebrew: *Me'ir*) the eyes of
the sages in *Halakhah*.[5]

The most widely known aphorism of Rabbi Meir is the one
cited in our *mishnah*. In various forms this insight has become a
truism of universal life and it may very well have been evoked
by an incident in Rabbi Meir's own life.

The Talmud records[6] that Rabbi Meir was ordained by
Rabbi Judah ben Bava and brings the objection: Surely he
received *Semikhah* (i.e., ordination as a rabbi) from his teacher
the revered Rabbi Akiva?. Yes, he did, but that ordination was
not accepted by his colleagues.

Perhaps one is tempted to say, that since Rabbi Akiva was a
descendent from converts and Rabbi Meir, as we stated, was
also a descendent from converts, that Rabbi Akiva, out of
compassion and sympathy conferred ordination upon his
student, Rabbi Meir. Impossible, Rabbi Akiva would never

commit such a misdeed.

Rashi offers us the correct answer. Rabbi Akiva's ordination was not accepted because Rabbi Meir was too young at that time. Thus, although he was the outstanding disciple of the most illustrious rabbi of the time, he was not recognized as a rabbinical authority because of his youth. Perhaps, in his justified resentment, Rabbi Meir might have said, "Do not judge me by my age, judge me by my knowledge! There may be a new flask, myself, filled with old wine - Torah."

Another explanation of Rabbi Meir's dictum may be that it was a reaction to the preceding[7] aphorism of Rabbi Jose ben Judah who advised against learning from the young, comparing it to eating unripe grapes or drinking freshly fermented wine. Rabbi Meir who had taught Torah from his youth tartly retorted: "A new flask may be filled with old wine and an old flask can be empty."

Another famous teaching that might have been a result of incidents in Rabbi Meir's own life is: "Just as one must recite a benediction over the good, so too must one bless the bad."[8] In another *mishnah*[9] we read that the blessing to be recited over evil tidings is "Blessed be the true judge."

Rabbi Meir lived during a turbulent era of Jewish history. It was the aftermath of the Bar Kokhba revolt which had failed, and the Roman oppressors adopted draconian methods to stamp out Judaism once and for all. Rabbi Meir witnessed the martyrdom of three *tannaim*: his revered teachers, Rabbi Akiva,[10] Rabbi Judah ben Bava[11] as well as his own father-in-law, Rabbi Hanina ben Teradion.[12] Also that of his mother-in-law.

His personal life was also filled with tragedy; his two sons died in childhood.[13] Yet, he retained his faith in God's justice to the extent that he could teach: "So must one bless the evil." When he stood at the bedside of his dead children, he proclaimed, "The Lord has given; the Lord has taken away; Blessed be the name of the Lord forever more!" A formula which has since entered the Jewish tradition as part of the burial service.

In contrast, one of his renowned teachers, Elisha ben Abuyah,[14] witnessed two tragic incidents, lost his faith, and became an apostate.[15] From that time he was referred to by his former colleagues as Aher, "The Other," and shunned. Rabbi Meir, however, continued to associate with him and even defended him in a discussion with Rabbi Judah, although without mentioning his name.[16]

On the verse, "You are sons to the Lord your God" (Deuteronomy 14:1), Rabbi Meir asserted that even a son who goes astray remains a son, and brought a proof from the verse in Hosea: "...and it shall be that instead of being said of them (Israel) 'they are not My people,' it shall be said of them 'they are the sons of the living God.'" (Hosea 2:1).

Many and touching are the accounts of conversations between Rabbi Meir and Elisha in which the disciple pleaded with his teacher to repent. Elisha refused claiming that he had heard a heavenly voice proclaiming, "Return, O backsliding children (Jeremiah 3:14); except Aher!"[17] Nonetheless, Rabbi Meir did not desist from his efforts to save Elisha and once, when the latter took to his sick bed, Rabbi Meir visited him and again pleaded for his eternal soul.[18] Again, Elisha insisted that his repentence would not be accepted. "No," said Meir, "for it is said in the Book of Psalms (40:3) You bring man to the brink of destruction and say: Return, O children of man."

At this, Elisha began to weep and died. Rabbi Meir was filled with rejoicing: "It seems to me that my teacher died while repenting!" Elisha's death had reminded Meir of the death of one, Eleazar ben Dordia.[19] This individual had led an immoral life and then heard a voice proclaim: "Just as a breathed breath will never return to its place, so too will Eleazar ben Dordia never be accepted in repentence!" At this, Eleazar was stricken with his guilt, and sat down with lowered head, wept and begged: "Mountains and hills. Plead for me!...Heaven and

earth! Pray for me!... Sun and moon! Intercede for me!" All
nature refused. "It all depends on me alone," said Eleazar and
putting his head between his knees he cried himself to death. At
that moment a heavenly voice was heard proclaiming "Rabbi
Eleazar ben Dordia is invited to his place in Paradise." On the
basis of this profound story, Rabbi Meir was certain that his
beloved teacher, Elisha ben Abuyah, who died while crying
was also forgiven and would take his place with the other great
sages in the Garden of Eden.

Many of his colleagues severely criticized Rabbi Meir for his
continued association with the apostate. The Talmud[20] records
the following encounter between Rabbah ben Shelah and
Elijah the Prophet:

"What is the Almighty doing at the moment?" inquired
Rabbah of Elijah.

"He is reviewing the traditions, each in the name of the
rabbi who stated them; except for the teachings of Rabbi
Meir because he was a pupil of Elisha ben Abuyah!"

"But Rabbi Meir found a pomegranate, (Elisha) ate the
fruit (Elisha's learning) and discarded the peel (Elisha's
heresies)."

"Since you plead for him the Almighty now announces,
Meir, My son says..."

Rabbi Meir's love of knowledge was so great that he was
prepared to learn from anybody, even a non-Jew. He had a
close Gentile friend, Abnimos Hagardi, who was an
outstanding philosopher.[21] When Abnimos' mother died,
Rabbi Meir visited him and found him in mourning, observing
a form of *Shiva*.[22] But when Rabbi Meir visited Abnimos after
his father's death he found him engaged in his normal
activities. Rabbi Meir was puzzled until Abnimos explained:
"In the Book of Ruth (1:8) we read, 'And Naomi said to her
two daughters-in-law, go! Return each of you to her mother's
home. May the Lord deal kindly with you as you have dealt
with the dead and with me!' Abnimos understood this to

mean that a child needs to mourn only its mother since Naomi mentioned only the "mother's home."

Jewish practice is, of course, to observe the mourning rites for both parents. Nonetheless, Abnimos' reply impressed Rabbi Meir, for the Gentile had "discovered" one of the sources for the law that a child's religious status follows its mother's and not its father's.

Rabbi Meir was a man of peace. When his personal dignity was involved, he was readily prepared to forego the honor due him, in order to avoid a conflict. However, where the honor of Torah was involved, he would accept no compromise. Two incidents reveal the first of these characteristics.

Rabbi Meir used to deliver a sermon every Friday evening. On one occasion he spoke longer than usual, and when one of the women in the audience came home she found that the lamps had burned out and her husband was very angry. "Where have you been?" he demanded. "I was at the rabbi's sermon," she answered. "Is that so! Well I swear an oath that I will not let you into this house until you go and spit in that rabbi's face." Rabbi Meir heard of what had happened and thought of a way to restore domestic peace for that unfortunate lady. He spread the word that he had an eye ailment and asked that any woman who knew how to recite the necessary incantation should come and cure him. Rabbi Meir was aware that the folk cure for eye ailments involved an incantation and expectoration into the sufferer's eye. The woman's neighbors realized that this was her opportunity and persuaded her to go to Rabbi Meir. He asked the terrified woman if she knew the cure and in embarrassment she confessed that she did not. "Never mind," said Rabbi Meir, "spit in my face seven times." After the poor woman had done the rabbi's will, he told her, Now, go to your husband and tell him: 'You told me to spit in the rabbi's face once, I did so seven times!'"[23]

Rabbi Meir's students were very disturbed at their teacher's behavior. Surely it is a degradation of the Torah for someone to spit in a sage's face. Rabbi Meir's reply was typical of his attitude: "Shall my honor be greater than the Almighty's? In the case of a woman who is suspected of infidelity by her husband, the law is that the name of God is written in a document which is erased by putting it into water. The woman then has to drink the water (Numbers 5:11-21). Thus, if the Almighty allows His name to be erased in an attempt to restore conjugal bliss, who am I not to permit a woman to spit in my face in order to bring peace to a family?"

On another occasion, a woman came to Rabbi Meir and told him that one of his students had married her, but she did not know which one. Thus, she fell into the category of an *agunah*, (i.e.), a woman whose husband is unknown or has disappeared. According to halakhah an *agunah* can never re-marry. Rabbi Meir immediately wrote a bill of divorce and gave it to her, as though he was the delinquent husband. Seeing their rabbi's action, all of his students followed suit, as Rabbi Meir had known they would. Since her "husband" was one of the students and she had received a divorce from each and every one, she was now freed from the bonds of *agunah* and could re-marry. Rabbi Meir, by his extraordinary deed had also saved the dignity of the student who was undoubtedly very embarrassed at the thought of having to step forward and admit his guilt.[24]

However, when he felt that the honor of the Torah was at stake, Rabbi Meir was uncompromising and this facet of his character is clearly revealed in his quarrel with Rabban Simeon ben Gamliel, the president of the Academy.

The custom in the Academy was that the entire assembly would rise when Rabban Simeon (the *Nasi*), Rabbi Natan (the *Av Bet Din*, the chief judge) or Rabbi Meir (the *Hakham*, the senior lecturer) entered, and remain standing until they were told to be seated. Rabban Simeon, intending to elevate the dignity of the *Nasi*, changed the procedure without consulting or informing either Rabbi Natan or Rabbi Meir. Under the new practice, when the *Nasi* entered the Academy, or any other gathering , all those assembled rose and remained standing until he sat down or asked them to be seated. When the *Av Bet Din* entered, three rows were to rise and remain standing until he passed, as one row sat down another rose so that three rows were to be standing as he passed. For the *Hakham* the assembly was to rise one row at a time. The next day Rabbi Natan and Rabbi Meir entered the Academy and upon confronting the new procedure, they departed in anger (for more details, see Chapter 13). In a dream which they both experienced, they were instructed to return to the Academy and apologize! Rabbi Natan did so, but Rabbi Meir refused, saying that he did not believe in dreams.[25]

As far as Rabbi Meir was concerned, the status and dignity of the office of *Hakham*, the main teacher of Torah, was involved, and he could not compromise. Had Rabban Simeon discussed the question with him prior to its implementation, Rabbi Meir would most probably have cooperated in order to find a way to enhance the office of *Nasi*. But he would not accept an arbitrary decision affecting the honor of Torah, no matter how high its source.

Rabbi Meir's wife was the famous Beruriah, whose father, Rabbi Hanina ben Teradim, was martyred.[26] Her mother was also killed and her sister was placed in a brothel. At Beruriah's request, Rabbi Meir set out to find her and redeem her from her shame. He did find her and offered the brothel keeper a huge bribe to let her escape. The guard refused to accept the bribe on the grounds that if the affair was discovered it would cost him his life. Rabbi Meir convinced him that if he was caught, all he would have to do was to say, "God of Meir save me!"and he would come to no harm. Unable to withstand the temptation, the guard agreed. The matter was discovered and as he was being led out to his execution, The brothel keeper recited the formula Rabbi Meir had taught him, The officials questioned him and he told them the whole story. He was released and a search was started for Rabbi Meir whose picture was posted at the entrances to the city with the legend: "This man is a wanted criminal." This might have been the first time in history that a "wanted" notice with a picture was posted! [27]

Rabbi Meir escaped his pursuers through a miracle which was based on the enormous reputation he enjoyed, even among his enemies. A Roman unit spotted him and chased after him. To escape, he darted into a known prostitute's house. The Roman commander did not search that house because it was inconceivable that Rabbi Meir would even enter such an establishment. According to another version, Rabbi Meir dipped his fingers into food being cooked by a non-Jew and then licked another of his fingers. The Romans, seeing their quarry apparently eating non-kosher food, assumed that he could not be Rabbi Meir and continued their search elsewhere. [27]

Rabbi Meir's stormy relations with his colleagues led to a very strange state of affairs that is evident even today in Talmudic literature.

In tractate Hullin, [28] a teaching is recorded that reveals Rabbi Meir's depth of psychological insight: "Rabbi Meir used to say 'A man should not invite his friend to dine if he knows he will refuse the invitation; nor should a man offer gifts to his friend if he knows they will not be accepted...'" Rabbi Meir considered such behavior as "stealing a person's mind" and, as such, a form of fraud. However, another of Rabbi Meir's dicta in the area of concern for a person's well-being suffered a strange fate. In *Avot D'Rabbi Natan,* [29] Rabbi Simeon ben Eleazar says in the name of Rabbi Meir: "Do not try to appease your friend while he is still angry. Do not try to comfort him while his dead lies before him. Do not visit him in the hour of his disgrace." The same *Mishnah* is taught in the Avot [30] but only in the name of Rabbi Simeon ben Eleazar without the mention of Rabbi Meir. Rabbi Simeon ben Eleazar was Rabbi Meir's most devoted disciple and most of his teachings come from Rabbi

Meir.

Rabbi Judah the Nasi, who was Rabbi Simeon ben Gamaliel's son and who redacted the Mishnah, must have known this; yet he decided to omit the reference to Rabbi Meir although it is a well-known rabbinical principle that "he who states a dictim in the name of its author brings salvation to the world."[31]

Rabbi Judah does not mention Rabbi Meir possibly because of Rabbi Meir's quarrel with Rabban Simeon ben Gamaliel, it was deemed that, in place of the accepted formula "Rabbi Meir said..." his laws were introduced with "Others say..." Furthermore, Rabbi Judah, when he does quote Rabbi Meir, uses an indirect form, it is said in the name of Rabbi Meir...[32]

However, there is also an element of poetic justice in the treatment meted out to Rabbi Meir. After all, he never quoted his own teacher, Rabbi Akiva, although he received many of his traditions from him.[33] But, the memory of Rabbi Meir is adequately preserved in the Talmudical dictum that, an anonymous *mishnah* is to be attributed to Rabbi Meir.[34]

Actually, Rabbi Judah the Nasi was ambivalent in his attitude to Rabbi Meir. On the one hand he said, "Had I sat in the Academy facing Rabbi Meir (i.e., as a student) instead of at his back, I would have been a far greater scholar than I am."[35] Yet, when Rabbi Meir died, Judah declared: "Let not the students of Rabbi Meir enter the Academy, for they do not come to learn but only to quibble..."[36]

In a sense, Rabbi Meir was too erudite. The Talmud records that his colleagues often disagreed with him because they could not fathom the depth of his reasoning. He could prove anything. even that the *sheretz*, the crawling insect, which is the absolute source of ritual impurity, was ritually pure, and vice versa.[37]

Rabbi Meir earned his living as a scribe and his exceptional scholarship is illustrated in the following incident. The law is that no matter how erudite a person is, he may not write or read any portion of the Holy Writ by heart, he must read or copy out of an authenticated text. However, when Rabbi Meir was visiting Asia Minor at Purim time and could not find a Scroll of Esther to read from, he wrote one from memory, which according to the Talmud,[38] was permitted to him only because of his great knowledge.

The *Midrash* however, explains this extraordinary feat in the following manner: Rabbi Meir wrote one Scroll from memory, checked it also from memory and then copied another from what he had written. He then read, the *Megillah*, from the second copy. Thus he was able to fulfill the letter of the Halakhah.[39]

It was in Asia Minor that Rabbi Meir died. His last wish was that he be buried in Eretz Israel, but until that could be arranged, he requested that his coffin be placed on the shores of the Mediterranean, for its waters also wash the shores of his beloved Eretz Israel.[40] In the folk tradition, however, his final resting place is in Tiberias, overlooking the Lake Kinneret not far from his revered teacher Rabbi Akiva.

Notes

1. *Avot* 4:27
2. *Gittin* 57b
3. *Maimonides' Mishnah Torah, Introduction*
4. *Gittin* 56a
5. *Eruvin* 13b
6. *Sanhedrin* 14a, *Rashi ad loc.*
7. *Avot* 4:26
8. *Berakhot* 48b
9. *Ibid* 54a
10. *Ibid*, 61b
11. *Sanhedrin* 14a
12. *Avodah Zarah* 17b
13. *Yalkut Shimoni to Proverbs* 31

14. *Hagigah* 15a
15. *TJ Hagigah* 2:1
16. *Kiddushin* 36a
17. *Hagigah* 15a
18. *TJ Hagigah* 2:1
19. *Avodah Zarah* 17a
20. *Hagigah* 15b
21. *Midrash Rabbah Genesis* 65:20
22. *Midrash Rabbah, Ruth* 2:13
23. *TJ Sotah* 1:4
24. *Sanhedrin* 11a
25. *Horayot* 13b
26. *Avodah Zarah* 17b
27. *Ibid*, 18b
28. *Hullin* 94a
29. *Avot D'Rabbi Natan* 29:1
30. *Avot* 4:23
31. *Megillah* 15a; *Avot* 6:6
32. *Horayot* 14a
33. *TJ Berakhot* 2:1
34. *Sanhedrin* 86a
35. *Eruvin* 13b
36. *Kiddushin* 52b
37. *Eruvin* 13b
38. *Megillah* 18b
39. *Midrash Rabbah, Genesis* 36:12
40. *TJ Killayim* 9:3 (end)